Tax

ATTACKS
AND
COUNTERATTACKS

Tax

ATTACKS

AND

COUNTERATTACKS

YOUR INDISPENSABLE GUIDE
TO
LONG-RANGE TAX STRATEGY

RICHARD A. WESTIN

AND

ALAN H. NEFF

HARCOURT BRACE JOVANOVICH

PUBLISHERS

San Diego   New York   London

Library of Congress Cataloging in Publication Data
Westin, Richard A., 1945–
Tax, attacks and counterattacks.
Includes index.
1. Tax planning—United States.   I. Neff, Alan H.
II. Title.
KF6297.W48   1983   343.7304   83-4353
347.3034
ISBN 0-15-188082-4

Designed by Robert Bull
Illustrations by Andy Myer

Printed in the United States of America

First edition

A B C D E

———

The Congress shall have power to lay and collect taxes on incomes, from whatever source derived, without apportionment among the several States, and without regard to any census or enumeration.
THE SIXTEENTH AMENDMENT TO THE CONSTITUTION
OF THE UNITED STATES OF AMERICA

Taxation without representation is tyranny.
JAMES OTIS

Representation without taxation is inconceivable.
THE AUTHORS

———

CONTENTS . . . .

For Liz, Meade, and our parents

Tax ATTACKS
AND
COUNTERATTACKS

Prologue

SEVERAL

HUNDRED

WORDS OF

EXPLANATION

ABOUT

TAX

PLANNING

IF YOU make enough money to pay taxes, you make enough to pay less. This book shows you how to do that.

It is completely up to date. It includes all the changes in the federal tax laws resulting from the 1981, 1982, and 1983 Congressional amendments. Even more important, it should have lifelong value because it explains basic tax strategies and ways to *think* about taxes, which will survive almost any foreseeable changes in our tax laws.

In the following pages, you will learn about tax planning, which is very different from tax deducting. There are any number of fine books about tax deductions, so we don't discuss them much.

Tax planning is much more powerful than tax deducting as a legal method to protect your hearth and home from taxation. By planning now to protect your future income from taxation, you can achieve a greater tax saving than by searching later for deductions against last year's income. In any event, you can and should use both strategies whenever legally possible.

Throughout the conception and writing of this book, two voices murmured in our ears. We listened carefully to both of them.

One voice said, "Keep it legal." We did, because we have no desire to expose you to the risks of unpleasant encounters with employees of the Internal Revenue Service. We're sure they're nice people and many of them have lovely families, but they have narrow interests that they aggressively pursue. Our suggestions are based on what the Internal Revenue Code intentionally encourages or permits in the ways and means of legal tax planning.

The other voice said, "Keep it light." We've always preferred to read technical materials presented by writers who use a soft touch whenever possible. It never hurts to put a little spin on the ball.

In short, the advice here is serious but the viewpoint is not. We hope this prevents some wear and tear on your attention span while you read.

Finally, there are two things you must have to make full use of our suggestions. You'll need a modicum of self-discipline and a bit of savings.

Planning requires discipline. You have to be willing to sacrifice some short-term pleasures to have resources to carry out your long-term decisions. You'll have to develop a regimen for your economic well-being and be willing to stick to it.

You'll also need an economic stake to get a good seat at the tax-planning table. Some of our advice will help people without any savings, but a great deal of what we discuss here will assist only those taxpayers who can hang on to a portion of their incomes and are willing to invest it. The amount doesn't really matter. We discuss investments that range from $50 to the sky's upper limit. The single connecting link is our belief that everything we explain can reduce your taxes.

No matter what you do with our advice, we want you to understand it. Take time to go through this primer carefully. The material is not difficult, but watch for several central concepts that appear and reappear. You should understand how they work.

CHAPTER *One*

► 1 THE

ORGANIZATION

OF THE

TAX WORLD

AND

A

PHILOSOPHICAL

JUSTIFICATION

FOR

TAX

PLANNING

(Just in Case

You Need One)

ON FEBRUARY 25, 1913, the Sixteenth Amendment became part of the Constitution of the United States of America. In thirty timeless words, the Amendment catalyzed the growth of American government.

There is a certain amount of public confusion about the organization of the Tax World. In a nutshell, here is how it works.

Congress writes the tax laws. After the president signs them, these legislative bills become part of the Internal Revenue Code (the Code).

The Treasury Department writes regulations to interpret the Code. Generally, the courts respect these regulations, but, if they are really wacky, judges will throw them out.

The Internal Revenue Service (the Service) is a bureau of the Treasury Department. The Service administers and enforces the tax laws and regulations and collects taxes. It also provides a system of internal appeals from its decisions that, for all the squawking about it, seems to be fair to most taxpayers.

If you don't like the IRS internal decision in your case, you can try to overturn it in either of two kinds of courts. You can go to the United States Tax Court or the general federal courts.

If you appeal through the Tax Court, you don't have to pay the disputed tax liability until and unless you finally lose. The Tax Court has nationwide jurisdiction and a streamlined small claims procedure when the amount in dispute is less than $5,000. There are about 50,000 cases on the Tax Court's docket.

If you want to appeal the IRS decision in the general federal courts (the U.S. District Courts and the U.S. Claims Court), you must first pay the disputed tax, demand a refund, and wait until you're certain you won't get the refund. These courts are also nationwide but have no simplified small claims procedures.

The Tax Court and general federal courts each have their own sets of precedents. Consequently, your particular appeal may do better in one kind of court than in the other. If you're going to appeal, your lawyer should do some research to determine which court will be more hospitable to your case.

One final note: Constitutional challenges to the tax laws are almost always a futile activity. You may be able to convince the Tax Court or federal court that a law or regulation should or shouldn't apply to you in a specific way, but you will probably never persuade a court to throw out the law or regulation. The Sixteenth Amendment is a very sturdy shield for almost every form of income taxation.

So much for civics. Lawyers, accountants, economists, cartoonists, editorial writers, and federal employees should say a daily prayer of thanksgiving for the Old Sixteenth. It has had the same salutary effect on their business affairs that the Eighteenth Amendment—the one that created Prohibition—had on the fortunes of organized crime.

The rest of us have not been so lucky. In fact, anthropologists have observed that since 1913 Americans have developed a ritual tax dance that follows the seasons.

Every winter, on our lunch hours, we stumble around in overheated bookstores, our overshoes dripping on the floors, and try to find the Ultimate Inexpensive Tax-Deductible Guide to Every Deduction in the Universe. Every spring, we use the Guide to play Find the Deduction Before April 15. Every summer, we sit on the beach, staring at the ocean, and the only thing on our minds is how we can keep the IRS from the door next year. Every fall, we . . . well, there's no point in going into additional painful detail. Most of us have danced The Dance many times; we've memorized the choreography.

Of course, there are people who don't worry about taxes. Most of them are very rich and avoid the anguish of taxes by simple methods; they arrange to have relatives leave them an inexhaustible supply of money (a brilliant strategy that we call Making Planning Moot) or they persuade other people to work hard, earn lots of money, and give it to them. The latter arrangement used to be called feudalism and is now called capitalism. Anyway, no matter which method the wealthy use, once they've got the money, they hire lawyers, accountants, and lobbyists to fend off the predatory omnivores of the IRS.

These minions free rich people to pursue their dearest interests, such as social renown for a good backhand passing shot. While they're on the courts, the rest of us must make up the federal budgetary deficit—or strive mightily to reduce by some minuscule portion our share of the burden.

There is no way to disguise the primary characteristics of that striving: it is a tedious and distasteful business to try to limit our taxes. We feel soiled and avaricious. Our self-esteem shrinks in direct proportion to the amount of time we spend on that task.

No matter what we do, we still have to slug it out, toe to toe, with the IRS. The odds favor the governmental Goliath, but we have our little slingshots. We ought to use them.

That leads us to the justification for this book. The wealthy can hire expensive tax advisors. You can't. Yet the Code was written to mete out justice for everyone.

THE RITUAL TAX DANCE

Upon very extensive study, the Code yields up some of its secrets, both in the form of highly specific rules, which no one can master in their entirety, and in a series of tax-planning implications that can be stated fairly briefly. We believe there are ten of them, and we hammer away at them throughout the rest of the book.

Unless you understand these ten principles, you will inevitably be reduced to the status of a mere deduction hunter—a low form of fiscal life. If you do learn the implicit principles, you will be able to *think* about tax planning. That is our mission in this book. You will only be learning what the Congress pretends you know already.

So much for our introduction. We realize you're hungry for content and details. Here they come.

CHAPTER *Two*

► 2 | THE

TEN

PRINCIPLES

OF

TAX

PLANNING

I don't believe in princerple,
But Oh, I du in interest.
J. R. LOWELL

To ENGAGE in effective tax plan-
ning, you must understand ten primary rules. After listing them,
we briefly discuss their meanings and consequences.

1. Balance your tax rates from year to year.
2. Defer your tax liability.
3. Substitute "above-the-line" deductions from income for "below-the-line" deductions.
4. Shift income from high-bracket taxpayers to low-bracket taxpayers.
5. Shift deductions from low-bracket taxpayers to high-bracket taxpayers.
6. Use current deductions, including depreciation, to produce long-term capital gains.
7. Leverage your investments.
8. Purchase property that is eligible for tax credits.
9. Avoid recapture.
10. Earn tax-free income.

► **1. BALANCE YOUR TAX RATES FROM YEAR TO YEAR**

This is a very simple proposition. It is critical to this primer and important to all taxpayers, but especially so to people who can expect their incomes to fluctuate from year to year. Attend carefully if you are self-employed, if your rate of compensation is highly variable, or if you suspect that you will be changing jobs regularly in the next few years.

Federal income taxation is "progressive" taxation. This is not a political description; it means that the tax rate is not a fixed percentage of your income no matter how much or how little you earn. In a system of progressive taxation, the more you earn, the larger the percentage of your income the federal government takes. The government may now collect as taxes as much as 50%

of your income. It used to be able to collect over 90%, and our present top rate of 50% is among the lowest in the modern world.

To put it mildly, progressive taxation is not a subject that elicits universal agreement about its virtues. Some people argue that it is *truly* progressive, because it imposes the heaviest burdens on those who can best afford to bear them. Other people don't like the arrangement because they say it discourages people from working harder and earning more money. If you want to read more about this debate, Milton Friedman, John Galbraith, George Gilder, Lester Thurow, and innumerable undergraduate economics majors have exhaustively explored the topic.

Practically everything that follows in this primer flows from this progressive characteristic of our tax laws. As they presently work, progressive federal tax rates make your tax bill larger if you are riding a roller coaster of taxable income instead of staying in roughly similar brackets from year to year. Consequently, you should avoid alternating substantial increases and decreases in income.

This seems obvious. *Of course* we should avoid unstable incomes. We don't know how you feel, but when our incomes rise and fall unpredictably, we tend to become unduly disturbed by trivial things, like spoons in the fork compartment of the silverware drawer or changes in the membership of Latin American juntas. There is no doubt about it; unstable incomes make us a little crazy.

These annual fluctuations in your income do not have to be large to be costly. Let's say you made $10,000 in 1979, $20,000 in 1980 (Nice going!) and $15,000 in 1981 (Well, nobody's perfect). If you were single, claimed one exemption, and took the standard deduction each year, your federal income tax liability (without social security taxes) would have been $1,182 in 1979, $3,829 in 1980, and $2,580 in 1981, for a total tax bill of $7,591 for the three years. That translates into an average annual tax rate of 16.9% on an income of $45,000.

Suppose instead that you made steadier levels of income; $13,000 in 1979; $17,000 in 1980; and $15,000 in 1981. You would have paid $1,849 in taxes in 1979, $2,913 in 1980, and $2,580 in 1981. Your tax bill would have been $7,342 on the same total income, with an average annual tax rate of 16.3%. You would have saved $249 by keeping your income more stable over the three years.

You would have saved even more if you had earned $15,000 in each of those three years. You would have paid $2,352 in taxes

BALANCING YOUR INCOME

in 1979, the same amount in 1980, and $2,580 in 1981. Your total tax bill would have been $7,284, at an annual rate of 16.2%, and you would have kept $307 of your income. You would also have noticed that your tax bill went up in 1981, even after the president and Congress "cut" your taxes. All they really did was to reduce the size of the increase in your taxes. That's life in Tax City.

The implications of all this talk of balancing are clear: try to anticipate and smooth out year-to-year fluctuations in income. If you expect a substantial change in your income next year, try to arrange the timing of your deductions so that they reduce the size of the change in your taxable income. If you expect your income to increase next year, defer deductions until next year. If you expect your income to decrease next year, try to take as many deductions as you can this year. Similarly, if you expect your *deductions* to increase next year, defer some income to next year. If your deductions will decrease next year, take more income this year.

We make all that sound very simple. We don't want you to think we're being glib. How *do* you defer or accelerate income or deductions? The answers are fairly well settled in the tax laws. Follow along while we play all the hits from that great revue, New Taxes of the 1980s.

► **2. DEFER YOUR TAX LIABILITY**

Deferral is the simplest tax-planning tool. It consists of deferring income, accelerating deductions, or both. The Internal Revenue Code encourages certain kinds of investments by saying that the IRS will not immediately tax the income you invest in them or the profit you make from them.

Tax deferral does not permanently relieve you of the duty to pay taxes on income you invest in or gain from these governmentally preferred activities. It is a means to delay your payment until it is more advantageous for you to give Washingtonians what they want. They don't mind. They're happy as long as you defer by the numbers. They know they'll get their share some day.

Deferring tax liabilities does not just involve deferring income into future years. It also includes accelerating deductions into the present year, consciously robbing them from the future.

The spectrum of tax-deferral practices is very broad. At the humble end of the spectrum, you can have your employer hold back some of your income until next year. Pension plans, which we discuss in more detail later, are principally tax-deferral plans. The portion of your income that you place in a pension plan will not be taxed until you withdraw it.

At the elegant end of the spectrum, you will find tax-deferral esoterica designed for people whose most difficult daily decision is whether to go to Paris or Rio for dinner. For that crowd, broker-age firms have various plans to offer, including things like cattle-breeding syndicates, which permit gargantuan deductions from income in one year. These kinds of investments also guarantee a corresponding elephantine increase in taxable income in the suc-ceeding year—unless you re-invest in the same venture or a similar enterprise. In these deals, you get to play with your money until you try to spend it. When that moment arrives, the IRS will want to collect its share.

As long as you stay on these gilded treadmills, the govern-ment leaves you alone. Unfortunately, treadmills become boring. You may have noticed that even hamsters have other interests. We hope you do, too. Keep that in mind when you consider such schemes. We discuss them later in detail.

► **3. SUBSTITUTE "ABOVE-THE-LINE" DEDUCTIONS FROM INCOME FOR "BELOW-THE-LINE" DEDUCTIONS**

This baffling terminology has a very simple meaning with impor-tant tax consequences. The distinction in name arises from the fact that there used to be a lined boundary on income tax forms that separated the places where you listed different kinds of deduc-tions. Go to the head of the class if you guessed that above-the-line deductions were listed above the line and—never mind.

There is a far more important distinction. Above-the-line de-ductions are wonderful things; you may *always* deduct them from your taxable income, and therefore they *always* reduce your tax liability. You want lots of above-the-line deductions. The more you have, the merrier you'll be at Tax Time.

Below-the-line deductions are comparatively feeble creatures. They will reduce your taxable income only when they exceed a certain amount (called the "zero-bracket amount," a fancy new term for what used to be called the "standard deduction") that the government calculates on the basis of your income and filing status (single, married filing separately, married filing jointly, or head of household).

Let's look briefly at the below-the-line deductions and then largely forget about them. They don't take us where we want to go.

BELOW-THE-LINE VS. ABOVE-THE-LINE DEDUCTIONS

Single taxpayers have a zero-bracket amount of $2,300. Married taxpayers who file separate returns each have zero-bracket amounts of $1,700. Married taxpayers who file joint returns share a zero-bracket amount of $3,400.

Therefore, a single taxpayer must have more than $2,300 of below-the-line deductions before those deductions from taxable income do a penny's worth of good. Likewise, that rare breed of married taxpayers who file separate returns must each have more than $1,700 in below-the-line deductions to justify using them rather than the standard deduction to reduce their taxable income. Married taxpayers who file joint returns must have a combined total of more than $3,400 in below-the-line deductions for those deductions to have any tax benefit.

Below-the-line deductions should now begin to sound very familiar. They are commonly called "itemized" deductions, and you put them on Schedule A of your tax return—if they are worth putting anywhere at all. They include interest payments on home mortgages and installment purchases, state and local taxes, medical and dental expenses, theft losses, and professional dues.

Your itemized below-the-line deductions are useless, useless, useless—unless their total exceeds the zero-bracket amount for your filing status. Put them out of your mind for now. We've got other things to talk about.

Because below-the-line deductions are also often called itemized deductions, above-the-line deductions are called "nonitemized" deductions. We can hear grammarians everywhere wincing. We *know* it's a terrible name, but there's nothing any of us can do about it. That's the way Tax People talk.

We hope you are now asking yourself, "How do I identify my nonitemized deductions so that I can make them fruitful and cause them to multiply?"—or words to that effect. The distinction between these two kinds of deductions is a bit blurry, but nonitemized deductions, or above-the-line deductions, or whatever you choose to call them, are usually business-related.

For example, interest on your home mortgage is an itemized deduction; the interest on the loan you obtain to purchase the automobile you use for business traveling is a nonitemized deduction. Consequently, this kind of auto loan interest always has tax value; you can always deduct the interest on the auto loan from your gross income. The interest on your home mortgage only has tax value if the total of your itemized deductions exceeds your zero-bracket amount.

We have now established an important point: nonitemized

deductions, which are generally business-related, always have tax value; itemized deductions, which are generally personal, may have no tax value. In other words, from a tax standpoint it is generally better to own a business than it is to own a home. If you value your safety, don't discuss this loudly in the presence of real estate brokers.

▶ **4. SHIFT INCOME FROM HIGH-BRACKET TAXPAYERS TO LOW-BRACKET TAXPAYERS**

and

▶ **5. SHIFT DEDUCTIONS FROM LOW-BRACKET TAXPAYERS TO HIGH-BRACKET TAXPAYERS**

We apologize. We assaulted and battered our style books and thesauri, but we couldn't find a more concise way to state these two principles. Fortunately for us, stating them this way makes their meaning fairly obvious.

These principles would be unnecessary if all incomes were subject to the same rate of taxation and there were no personal or business deductions from income. Because that isn't the case, we have to find ways to put ourselves in more tolerable tax brackets.

Using these two principles, there are three ways to put yourself in a lower bracket:

□ have someone in a lower bracket earn and report income you would have to report;

□ have someone in a lower bracket provide you with deductions they don't need; or

□ use both methods.

Consequently, your tax plan should establish these kinds of symbiotic relationships with taxpayers in brackets lower than yours. Shift income to them and take deductions from them.

There are three primary vehicles for establishing this symbiosis: your family, your business, and your investments. In later sections and chapters, we explain in detail how to use each of them. At this point, we simply state several important facts.

First, the tax laws permit you to arrange your family's income to take advantage of different rates of taxation for each family member. If you follow the rules, you may legally move income to low-bracket family members and take deductions from them. The simplest example is hiring family members in your business. They get the income. Your business gets the deduction for their salary and benefits.

Second, the basic types of business organization (corporations, partnerships, and sole proprietorships) are taxed differently. Corporations are generally taxed more gently than partnerships or sole proprietorships. If you're a high-bracket taxpayer or have a second income, you may be able to create a corporation that will serve as your low-bracket taxpayer. You'll be able to protect income in it and take deductions from it.

Finally, the tax laws encourage many kinds of investments that can assume the same role as family members and businesses. We discuss these investments in later chapters.

► **6. USE CURRENT DEDUCTIONS, INCLUDING DEPRECIATION, TO PRODUCE LONG-TERM CAPITAL GAINS**

This principle has two meanings. First, it means that you should try to realize your income in the form of long-term capital gains. Second, at the same time, you should try to keep the expenses that you incur in obtaining your gains fully deductible. This is called "conversion," and it is far less complicated than it initially sounds. Follow along.

The Internal Revenue Code basically distinguishes between two kinds of income: ordinary income and capital gains. Ordinary income consists of the money, goods, or services you receive for the things you do or make for other people. It may be special to you, but it's ordinary to the Internal Revenue Service.

Ordinary income is subject to progressive taxation; the more you get for your labors, the more tribute you must give to Washington. You may be required to give the IRS as much as 50% of your ordinary income. You could say that ordinary income is subject to extraordinary taxes.

A capital gain is the income you get from the sale or exchange of property you've purchased and held for investment or business use for a specific period of time. If you own the property for at least a year and a day and sell it for more than it cost you, you get a long-term capital gain. Generally, if you own the property for a shorter period of time and sell it for a profit, you have a short-term capital gain.

The two kinds of gains are taxed differently. We discuss long-term gains now and short-term gains in the chapters on corporations and securities.

Long-term capital gains have one very significant characteristic. They are taxed at a much lower rate than ordinary income. Sixty percent of any long-term capital gain is automatically excluded from income. The remainder is taxed at the same progressive rate that applies to your ordinary income. In other words, you will not pay a tax on your capital gain in excess of 20% of the gain. This happens because the maximum tax rate on ordinary income is now 50%. Fifty percent of the taxable 40% of your gain is 20%, no matter how many times you try to reach a different result.

Suppose you purchased 100 shares of Fred's Storm Door Company at $50 a share for a grand total of $5,000. One year and one day later, you sold your shares for $6,000. Your capital gain is $1,000. You may immediately exclude 60% of your gain from your income tax return. That's your reward for guessing right about Fred's stock.

The remaining $400 goes into the pot with your ordinary income. The $400 gain is taxed at the rate that applies to your total taxable income. If your taxable income puts you in the 20% bracket, you owe the government $80 of your gain. If you're in the 50% bracket, you owe the government $200 of your gain. No matter how large your income, you get to keep at least $800 of the $1,000 you made from the sale of your shares. At worst, you keep 80% of *any* long-term capital gain, while you may only keep as much as 50% of your taxable ordinary income.

It should be painfully clear that from a tax standpoint, long-term capital gains are preferable to ordinary income. Now you know why the Feds call it "ordinary" income.

Back to conversion. Conversion is the means by which you make a capital gain more valuable. In essence, you purchase property that you expect will produce a capital gain someday and arrange to have the expenses of holding that property fully and currently deductible. You then use the expenses to wipe out the ordinary income from the property (if it produces any) and other ordinary income. At some later time, you sell the property for more than you paid for it and you take a capital gain.

An example: Let's assume you are in the 50% tax bracket. You decide to buy some vacant land for $50,000, expecting it to increase in value. You pay $10,000 in cash and borrow $40,000 for one year at 15% to finance the balance. During the next year, you pay $6,000 interest on the loan and you have no other expenses.

This interest can be deducted below the line. You have incurred at least $6,000 worth of itemized deductions that we assume you can fully use to reduce your taxable income.

One year and one day later, you sell the land for $55,000. You recover your $10,000 investment, pay off the loan, and have a capital gain of $5,000. You exclude $3,000 of the gain and pay the appropriate tax on the balance, which in no event will exceed $1,000. That means you pocket $4,000 of the $5,000 gain.

Your original investment, which returned intact, cost you $6,000 in interest expenses but saved you $3,000 in taxes, and has produced at least $4,000 in tax-free income for a net after-tax gain of $1,000. Most people in their right minds would consider that a satisfactory after-tax return on $10,000 invested for one year.

You may be wondering why $6,000 in deductions saved only $3,000 in taxes. The reason is simple. In the 50% bracket, each time you earn $2.00, you owe $1.00 in taxes. Likewise, if you deduct $2.00, you save $1.00 in taxes. So, if you deduct $6,000, you save $3,000. The lower your bracket, the smaller your tax savings.

Now that you understand straightforward conversion, you are ready to learn what depreciation is and how it can be used to convert ordinary deductions into capital gains.

. . . .

A Short Discourse on Depreciation

Grow old along with me!
The best is yet to be, . . . ROBERT BROWNING

With astute perception, Congress has observed that nothing lasts forever. It has enshrined this fatalistic principle of pre-determined decay in our tax laws, in the concept of depreciation. Universities that offer accounting courses could subtitle them "Fun with Depreciation," and not run afoul of truth-in-advertising laws.

Depreciation can only be claimed for business and investment property—and never for land. We can ruin land (we do it all the time), but we can't depreciate it.

In its simplest form, depreciation works this way. You purchase a piece of business property, let's say an electric typewriter, for $200. Typewriters are pretty sturdy devices, but like the rest of us they get old and decrepit. After a while, your typewriter stops working altogether, and your typewriter service representative pronounces it dead. Given normal wear and tear, we'll assume that this depressing process takes five years, the "expected useful life" of typewriters.

The tax laws let you divide the cost of the typewriter by five and deduct the result from your profits from doing business with the typewriter each year, until you've deducted the entire cost of the typewriter. If the typewriter cost $200 and will last five years, you get to "write off" $40 each year from the profits of the business in which you use your typewriter. That is "straight-line" or garden-variety depreciation. In effect, the government allows you to recover 100% of the cost of the typewriter.

Accountants *love* depreciation. They've devised more variations on that basic straight-line theme than blues musicians could ever make from a 1-4-5 chord progression. Some of the variations deduct most of the depreciation in the value of the property in the first years of ownership; some methods place it toward the end of the expected useful life of the property. The common element in all depreciation is that you *must* stick to the timetable you establish for the property.

The tax law changes in 1981 made the rules governing depreciation incredibly generous, giving the business world a big break. The government renamed depreciation "cost recovery" and now lets you fix the rate of depreciation according to several lists that constitute the "Accelerated Cost Recovery System" (ACRS). We'll just stick with "depreciation."

The accent in ACRS is on the word "accelerated." The government sped up depreciation schedules so that business people can completely recover the cost of the property in shorter periods of time than they could before. This means they write off much larger hunks of the purchase cost of business property over a shorter period of years. They thereby reduce the amount of their taxable profits over the depreciation period by more in each single year than they ever could before.

Every kind of new or used tangible business property acquired after 1980 may be placed on one of four basic schedules: three years, five years, ten years, or fifteen years. The ACRS schedules are pretty absurd. For example, buildings can be *completely* written off in fifteen years. When was the last time someone told you a new building would go to pieces in fifteen years? Would you buy a new home that had that kind of expected life?

The picture we've just painted is simple and clear. You buy a piece of property and use it for your business until you've used it up. At that point, you have written its cost down to $0, and you throw it away. Each year you used it, you wrote off a portion of the purchase price to reduce your income.

Unfortunately, economic matters in the real world aren't always that simple. Many businesses and investors replace used depreciable property with new property and resell the old property before they've completely written it off. In many cases, property that is completely written off is still useful and can be resold for scrap parts or further use.

When depreciated property is resold, the resale may produce taxable income. The income may be taxed as ordinary income, capital gains, or some of both. The outcome depends on five factors:

□ the kind of property;
□ the depreciation schedule you chose;
□ the amount of depreciation you've claimed;
□ the price you originally paid for it; and
□ the price you get for your property when you resell it.

There are tons of tax regulations in this area, but really only three important things to learn right now:

□ If you resell property for more than its current depreciated value (which is called its "adjusted basis") but less than you originally paid for it, the difference will be taxed as ordinary income or a capital gain, depending on what kind of property you are selling.
□ If you resell property held over a year for *more* than you paid for it, the difference between the price you paid and the resale price is *always* taxed as a capital gain, unless you deal in this property as a regular business.
□ Resales of "improved" real estate depreciated on a straight-line basis are taxed more gently than resales of *any other form of property depreciated on any kind of schedule.* "Improved real estate" is land with some sort of structure on it (a building, a barn, a bridge, anything). The structure is what you get to depreciate, *not* the land.

For now, that's all you need to know about the taxation of resales of depreciated property. Two simple examples show how this works:

1. Let's suppose you do purchase a brand new $200 typewriter for your business. You depreciate it on a five-year straight-line schedule. After five years, you've written it down to an adjusted basis of zero.

If you give the typewriter away, there is no taxable income from the transaction. If you sell it for any price from one cent to $200, the difference between the resale price and the typewriter's adjusted basis of zero is taxed as ordinary income. If you sell it for *more* than $200, the first $200 is taxed as ordinary income and any amount over $200 is taxed as a capital gain.

With one exception, this is the way the rules work for any kind of real estate or tangible business or investment property depreciated on any kind of schedule. As we mentioned, the one key exception is improved real estate depreciated on a straight-line schedule.

2. Let's suppose you buy a new duplex for $200,000. You depreciate it on a fifteen-year straight-line schedule. At the end of the fifteen years, when the adjusted basis of the duplex is zero, you resell it. The *entire* amount you receive from the resale is taxed as a capital gain. No portion of it is taxed as ordinary income. That's one reason why improved real estate can be a great long-term investment.

These rules also govern resales of depreciated property when it is resold before it is completely written off. If you sold the typewriter after three years of straight-line depreciation, the adjusted basis would be $80. If you sold it for any amount from $80.01 to $200.000, the difference would be taxed as ordinary income. If you sold it for more than $200, $120 would be taxed as ordinary income and the excess over $200 would be taxed as a capital gain.

The duplex would also be treated as it was in the earlier case. After three years of straight-line depreciation, its adjusted basis would be $160,000. If you sold it for any price more than its adjusted basis, the difference would be taxed as a capital gain. If you depreciated it on an accelerated basis, and sold it for more than $160,000, much of the first $40,000 of the difference would be taxed as ordinary income. If you sold it for more than $200,000, most of the first $40,000 would be taxed as ordinary income and the excess over $200,000 would be taxed as a capital gain. We are deliberately avoiding delving into this deeply. Explaining how one arrives at the "most of" number is very time-consuming and more than a mite dull.

When you purchase *any* kind of business or investment property, you should be aware of what can happen when you resell it.

Unless you want to accelerate income, you don't want a lot of ordinary income from resales of property pouring on to your tax return. If you're in possession of your sanity, you will always want capital gains from resales (or nothing at all).

In other words, depreciation can be a two-edged sword. It can nick you when you do well selling depreciated property.

These rules make sense. The government is telling you that the property really didn't depreciate to the extent you claimed. The government reclaims the unwanted depreciation as ordinary income or capital gains.

That takes care of this digression. Let's get back to conversion.

. . . .

A few pages ago, you purchased a piece of land for $10,000 of your own and $40,000 belonging to someone else. That worked pretty well, so let's take your original $10,000, plus your after-tax capital gain of $4,000 (we've decided you're in the 50% bracket, you poor devil), and embark upon another economic adventure.

You invest your $14,000 in a two-apartment brownstone that costs $140,000. You borrow $126,000 on a thirty-year interest-only mortgage to cover the balance of the purchase price.

The rents from the two apartments are just enough to cover your mortgage interest expense, and maintenance costs for the building. As a result, you don't pay a cent to carry the building. Your tenants do it for you. You do claim straight-line depreciation deductions of $9,333.33 dollars in each year that you own the building ($140,000 divided by 15 equals $9,333.33). Consequently, you reduce your tax bill by $4,666.67 a year, because depreciation deductions are subtracted from your taxable income and are therefore tied to your tax bracket. To put it another way, in your 50% bracket, each dollar of the deduction means 50 cents of taxes saved. Another point: the depreciation deduction is purely on paper. No cash changes hands. It is purely in the imagination.

At the end of fifteen years, you sell the building for $140,000, exactly what you paid for it. By now, you've depreciated the building to zero, so your long-term capital gain is $140,000, but you have to pay off the $126,000 loan. That leaves you $14,000 in cash and a tax bill for your capital gain.

What's the result of all this? You've paid off the $126,000 loan, and had $9,333.33 a year in depreciation deductions for fifteen years that reduced your taxable income by $4,666.67 each year. You protected $70,000 from the Treasury Department ($4,666.67 times 15 years).

You do have to pay 20% of the $140,000 capital gain back to the government in long-term capital gains taxes (i.e., $28,000), but that is cheap at the price and way down the road of time. To put it another way, the whole thing saved you $42,000 in taxes ($70,000 minus $28,000), a pretty fair return on a $14,000 investment.

We'll admit right here that we've painted a slightly rose-tinted picture. If your building is in good physical condition, it's likely that rent won't cover all the expenses, at least not right away. If the building is good, its value may double in fifteen years. That's the rate at which real estate has appreciated in recent years. Even if your expenses are more than your rents, the profit from the resale will cheer you up, because it's taxed at the rates that apply to long-term capital gains (if you use straight-line depreciation). The rosy coloration of this example is basically appropriate.

This illustration depicts the way things really work for rich investors, assuming you add one or more zeros to each figure in the example. The point is that the same strategies are available to moderately affluent investors.

Several things should be obvious. First, as we said before, you need a stake to get into the game. It need not be a large one, but you must have enough to convince a lender to join you and enough assets to protect the lender if you default. Second, you must be able to predict with some certainty that you will get deductions you can use. Otherwise, there's no value to the purchase beyond the capital gain. Finally, you've got to do this with a reliable investment, something you're fairly certain will appreciate.

► 7. LEVERAGE YOUR INVESTMENTS

"Leverage" is another one of those linguistic abominations that plague the investment world. If you've been in any businessmen's locker room in the last few years, you've heard people throw it around like used towels. Financial types, like computer people, derive inexplicable satisfaction from fooling around with the language when hardy old-fashioned American words would do just as well. Overnight, a perfectly serviceable noun like "leverage" becomes a verb. We know these changes are a tribute to the marvelous plasticity of the American language, but sometimes we get a little depressed.

Anyway, leveraging is borrowing money to increase the

amount of property you can hold. That's all. That's the whole idea.

In the last example, you leveraged your investment in real estate by borrowing $126,000. Without leverage, you could have held only $14,000 worth of property.

A large number of financial planners think that leverage is the key to wealth in an inflationary economy. They may be right, but they're also the folks who made leverage a transitive verb. Your guess is as good as ours.

By the way, you can breathe more easily now. We're over the hump; from here on, it's all downhill.

▶ **8. PURCHASE PROPERTY THAT IS ELIGIBLE FOR TAX CREDITS**

This is only the second time you've seen the words "tax credit" in this book, right? Right. It's an easy concept to understand.

After you've taken all your itemized and nonitemized deductions, you're left with your taxable income, which we fervently hope is very, very small. You turn to the tax tables and discover the amount of the tax on your income.

At this point, you get to reduce your taxes further if you have tax credits. You may directly subtract from your tax bill a percentage of the purchase price of certain goods and services that the government encourages you to buy. Credits also include income taxes withheld by your employer, part of the cost of child care, energy tax credits, tax payments on foreign income, and investment tax credits. By the way, the category of tax credits also includes contributions to political candidates, who are often selling you a bill of goods for a service of dubious value.

For our discussion here, we will focus on the investment tax credit, sometimes called the ITC. The investment tax credit, like most things, is not quite what its name implies it is. It is *not* a tax credit for *all* kinds of investment. It ought to be called a "credit for the purchase of tangible business property other than real estate." When you buy certain business property that the government wants you to purchase, you may deduct from your tax bill a percentage of the price of that property.

There is a catch. You must keep the property for a specific minimum period of time or the government will require you to repay some or all of the credit. The percentage of the purchase price you may deduct from your tax bill and the amount of time you must keep the property vary with the kind of property you buy. Some kinds of property are eligible for a 6% credit and must be held for a minimum of three years to have full credit. Other kinds of property are eligible for a 10% credit and must be held for five years for full credit. In all cases, you earn the credit at the rate of 2% of the purchase price for each year you hold the property.

For example, if you pay $10,000 for a car that you will use exclusively for business purposes, you may immediately subtract 6% of the purchase price of the car—$600—from your tax bill for the year in which you bought it. It's as if the government paid 6% of your car. Actually, other taxpayers *without* investment tax credits are paying for that 6%. That's a sweet deal, but it suggests more about the relationship between Washington and Detroit than we care to go into here.

To retain full credit for the car, you must keep it for three years, because cars are on the 6%/three-year schedule. If you sell if after one year, you must repay the government two-thirds of your $600 credit. If you sell it after two years, you must repay one-third of the credit.

You don't owe any interest, however, on the repayment. That is why reclaimed tax credits are often called "tax-free loans from the government." You get cash savings against your tax bill when you claim the credit. If you get rid of the property before you earn the full credit, you just repay the part to which you weren't entitled.

There's no magic to determining what kind of credit you may claim. The government describes the categories of property eligible for credit, the percentage of the credit, and the period over which you earn it. But there is a small catch. If you're planning to depreciate your property, you may not be able to use the full price of the property as the beginning point for your depreciation schedule. Nowadays, you have to make a choice between either (1) a full credit, but with a reduction in the amount you can write off, or (2) a reduced credit, with no reduction in the amount you can write off.

In the car example we just used, if you use the first alternative (full credit) your price for purposes of depreciation is $9,700. That's the total of depreciation deductions you may take over the period you hold the car.

If, instead, you wanted to write off the full $10,000, you could only claim a 4% credit (i.e., $400). If the property happened to qualify for a 10% credit and you wanted to write off the full cost, you could only claim an 8% credit.

We can't tell you which alternative is better for you. You'll only know after consulting someone with sharp pencils and a green eyeshade. If you want our guess, we would vote for taking the full credit as the better deal.

Investment tax credits are more available now than they have ever been. Anytime you purchase property for your business, you ought to find out whether you can get a tax credit for the purchase and how large the credit will be.

If you carefully play by the rules that govern investment tax credits, you are transported into the most privileged of economic classes. You join farmers who get paid to grow nothing at all, other farmers who get price supports for their tobacco crops and dairy products, and everyone associated with the maritime industry, no matter how remote their relationship to it.

In short, you have entered the government's most exclusive and attractive theme park: Subsidyland. We hope you enjoy your visit.

► **9. AVOID RECAPTURE**

In the sections on conversion and investment tax credits, we mentioned two things of which you have to be aware. If you sell depreciated property for more than its adjusted basis (original cost minus depreciation), the government will tax the difference. The important question is whether it will be taxed as ordinary income or capital gains. Similarly, if you purchase property, take an investment tax credit, and sell the property before you've earned the full credit, you'll have to pay back the unearned portion of the credit.

Those are cases of recapture. The government "recaptures" the depreciation you shouldn't have taken, because the property was worth more than you said it was. The government "recaptures" the unearned portion of the investment tax credit because you didn't hold it long enough.

However, the recapture will be one-for-one. There is no interest or penalty attached to recapture. The result is the tax-free loan from the government we mentioned earlier.

The tax laws could add penalties to recapture, but it wouldn't be economically or socially sensible. Penalties would discourage investment in new and more efficient equipment and would undermine the concept of depreciation. Congress has decided to avoid the havoc by taxing recaptured depreciation and investment tax credits as current income.

That leaves us with one more principle to discuss. We told you to "earn tax-free income" and now we'll tell you why.

► **10. EARN TAX-FREE INCOME**

There are two kinds of tax-free income: tax-exempt income and imputed income. Tax-exempt income is explicitly exempted by the Internal Revenue Code. Imputed income is exempted by administrative action of the IRS. Imputed income is income that the government has decided not to tax, because by its nature it's too hard to figure out what it's worth. The hidden reason for the decision is that if it were taxed there would be a revolution. Imputed income constitutes the nonfinancial benefits that you get from your activities and the property you own.

Let's suppose you have a job that you really enjoy. The government can figure out how much salary you make and tax it. They can't figure out the value of the pleasure you take from doing your job. If they could, they might tax it. They can't, so they don't.

Let's take another example. Suppose you own a boat. Part of the year you rent it out to the public. You collect income, you subtract the deductible expenses of owning and maintaining the boat, and you pay taxes on whatever's left. The rest of the year, you use the boat yourself. You don't pay taxes on the pleasure you get from using the boat. Other common examples are homegrown food, cutting your own firewood, occupying the home you own, and services provided for free by friends and relatives.

In short, your overall goal is two-fold: minimize taxable income by all the methods we've mentioned and maximize tax-free income. Plan your income and taxes so you can enjoy what you do and own.

► **THE COMPLETE ALL-NATURAL UNEXPURGATED MEANING OF THE TEN PRINCIPLES**

Ultimately, all of these strategies direct you to do the following:

☐ Balance your tax rates from year to year by deferring or accelerating income and deductions.
☐ Establish symbiotic relationships with taxpayers in lower brackets than yours to take deductions from them and shift income to them.

☐ Minimize ordinary income and maximize capital gains and tax-free income.

Congratulations! You may not believe it, but you've learned all of the basic principles of tax planning. Unless Congress enacts a flat-rate tax and repeals all deductions, these principles will always work for you. The rest of this book is devoted to their application in your work, investments, and play.

Take a break. You've earned the rest.

CHAPTER

▶ 3 OF

TIME

AND

TAXES:

STRATEGIES

FOR

TIMING

INCOME

AND

DEDUCTIONS

My object all sublime I shall achieve in time.

W. S. GILBERT

MOST OF US naturally assume that the best way to reduce tax liability is to defer income as long as possible and take deductions as soon as possible. Unlike Shoeless Joe Jackson, you now can say that it ain't so. The tax consequences of fluctuating income discussed in Chapter Two make that clear.

You will usually want to defer income and accelerate deductions, but it is sometimes true that income should be recognized early and deductions should be deferred. If you expect your income to increase next year, try to move some of your income into this year and defer as many deductions as you can until next year. That will reduce your taxes over the two-year period.

To do this most easily, you must be someone accountants call a "cash method" taxpayer. Cash method taxpayers recognize and report income when they actually receive it and expenses when they pay them. Most of us are cash method taxpayers; if you aren't, you are very strange and you will know it.

How can cash method taxpayers time income and deductions? There are very simple methods to accelerate and defer income and deductions.

► **ACCELERATING INCOME**

First, you can sell your future income. For example, if you own a share of stock, you can sell your right to future dividends. You recognize income immediately from the sale, and the gain is taxed as ordinary income.

You can do this with any kind of debt. If you are owed money on accounts from sales of goods or services in your business, you can sell those obligations and recognize ordinary income on the spot. If you own property that you lease to someone, you can sell the lease to your tenant or someone else and then you will receive immediately taxable income.

You can also try to convince your employer to pay you

slightly more this year and reduce your income in the next year. Then again, Tom Thumb could get a job as a guard in the National Basketball Association. Employers aren't very receptive to the idea of paying you more in this year and less in the next. They can't be sure you'll still be around next year.

► **DEFERRING DEDUCTIONS**

It's also relatively easy to defer deductions, which you'll want to do if you know your income will rise next year. One obvious way to defer deductions is to be slow in paying your bills. You may not make your creditors happy, but then again, they may be looking for ways to defer income. Remember, almost everybody's doing the Tax Dance.

Delayed payment of debt is a strategy frequently used by people near the end of their tax years (or their ropes). Delaying payment of December bills until January can make a big difference in your tax liability.

For example, you might not pay your real estate taxes for this year until next year. However, this strategy may fail because you might have to pay a penalty, which would wipe out the benefit and is *not* deductible, or an interest charge, which *may* be deductible, to local tax agencies.

If you own investment property, you can defer repairs on it or the payment of premiums on your insurance for the property. You probably won't want to do this, however, if deferral of the repairs or insurance payments reduces the value of the property or would cause your insurance to lapse.

Basically, any expenditure can be deferred. The questions you have to answer are whether your creditors will tolerate deferral and whether there are other risks of the kinds discussed so far.

The other primary ways to smooth out your income are to defer income and accelerate deductions. It's relatively easy to defer income, but hard to accelerate deductions, because the IRS is hostile to that strategy.

► **DEFERRING INCOME**

You can use several methods to defer your income. You can have your employer pay less for your services this year and more in subsequent years. Employers like this a lot more than paying more for your work now and less later (again, because they can't be sure you'll be around next year). Professional athletes and other high-income celebrities do this whenever they can. The press describes these arrangements as "deferred compensation contracts," and we discuss them in more detail in Chapter Five.

If you sell goods or your property, the tax laws let you use a very straightforward income-deferral technique. It's the installment sale. If you sell property to someone who pays you the full price in installments over an extended period of time, you need only report the gain as the payments are made.

The installment technique is now automatically available to almost everyone. You don't have to make any official declarations of any sort to qualify for it. To protect yourself, make sure you have the terms of the sale in a written contract between you and your buyer. You want to be able, if necessary, to prove to the IRS that you're doing this. You also ought to have a written contract in case your buyer breaches the agreement and you want to sue to enforce its terms.

DEFERRING YOUR INCOME

There can be complications in installment sales. The calculation of your taxable income is somewhat more complex if you and your buyer finance the transaction with some type of mortgage, but the basic idea remains the same; you stretch the period in which you recognize your gain.

These are also legal limits on the use of installment sales. For example, you cannot sell property to your spouse on an installment plan. The IRS will treat that as a sham and hold you liable immediately for the full price of the sale. You *can* use installment sales with other relatives, but you must have a genuine installment arrangement.

► **ACCELERATING DEDUCTIONS**

It is more difficult to accelerate deductions. Of course, you can pay for deductible installment purchases at a faster rate than your creditor requires. You can also make repairs on investment property earlier than you may need to make them. You can undertake major itemizable expenses now rather than later. For example, a child's teeth can be a very expensive family obligation. You might decide to burden your child with braces this year rather than next. You can also prepay your state income and property taxes.

In all of these examples of accelerated deductions, you must be contractually obligated to pay for the services and property. If the IRS concludes you have just made some sort of refundable deposit, you will lose the deduction.

► **INCOME AVERAGING**

There is one last strategy that deserves separate discussion because it apparently flies in the face of everything said so far about smoothing your income. It is income averaging, a special elective device that you calculate on Schedule G on the 1040 form. It can be very beneficial, but it's difficult to control.

The theory of income averaging is simple. If your income has increased sharply this year, the government allows you to pay reduced taxes this year and larger "phantom" taxes for the previous four years. In other words, Congress recognizes the tax consequence of income fluctuation. You may legally pretend that the dramatic increase in your income did not occur this year but was spread smoothly over this year and the previous four years.

That's a very rough description of income averaging. It is not easy to plan for income averaging. The calculations can be difficult because they're based on income you expect to receive next year. Very few of us can predict that with certainty. Very few of us can predict *anything* with certainty.

If you can expect a sharp increase in income next year, then you should go to the IRS to get a Schedule G, sit down, and work it out yourself. The Schedule and instructions are very clear, but you will need copies of your earlier years' tax returns at your side.

There are limitations on the use of income averaging. First, you can't have been anyone's dependent during any of the previous four years. If someone claimed you as a dependent during any of those years, you forfeit your right to average your income. (There is a minor exception to that rule, mentioned very soon.) Second, the upward fluctuation in your income must be very sharp. The measure of sufficient sharpness is called the "averageable income." The averageable income is not a fixed feature for all taxpayers. It is a function of your own income during the five-year period multiplied and divided by several constants.

There are some other important limitations on using this device. Your averageable income must exceed $3,000. You must be a citizen or resident of the United States during the computation year. Corporations, estates, and trusts cannot average income. You must provide 50% or more of your economic support during each of the four years in your base period, unless you're at least twenty-five years old during the fifth year and have not been a student during at least four years since you turned twenty-one. You do *not* lose the right to average for years in which you are unemployed. There are also some limitations when some of your income comes from certain kinds of trusts or early withdrawal from certain kinds of pension plans.

In other words, your particular financial circumstances may make the matter more complex. It's best to sit down and figure out whether you'll be able to do it, *before* the year in which you expect to strike it rich. You can always average income in the year in which your income increases. You can even do it afterward, by filing an amended return for the averageable period.

By preparing a trial return before your peak-income year, you gain an additional advantage. You may discover that you won't be able to average *unless* you reduce your income in the year *preced-*

ing the big increase in your income. You've seen how to reduce your income in any given year: you accelerate your deductions and defer income to the year in which you expect to do well. Of course, this will also increase any benefit you can expect to derive from averaging.

CHAPTER  *Four*

4 | DEFERRING

INCOME:

IRAs,

KEOGHS,

AND

TAX-SHELTERED

ANNUITIES

———

Be wise today, 'tis madness to defer.
E. YOUNG

———

Unless you stopped reading newspapers several years ago, you know that there's been a major topographical rearrangement of the Wonderful World of Pensions. Before we go any further, we'll admit right now that, for most of us, pensions are a pretty boring subject. After all, we're charter members of the Now Generation, the survivors of the Me Decade. Do we care about retirement income? Nah! We don't have time for that; we've got hang-gliding lessons in an hour!

A very significant thing happened in the late seventies, while many of us were teaching our dogs to catch Frisbees. Middle-income taxpayers, scared by rumors of the impending bankruptcy of the Social Security system and a raftload of financial inter-mediaries (banks, savings and loan associations, insurance com-panies, and the like), persuaded Congress to change the tax laws governing pensions and other forms of retirement income.

In the bad old days, the extraordinary tax advantages of pen-sion plans were available only to employees of large corporations. Professionals and sole proprietors prodded Congress into extend-ing those benefits to them. Congress even authorized new forms of pension planning for individuals already covered by major cor-porate pension plans.

Alert soul that you are, you're asking yourself, "What are these dazzling 'benefits'?" The most obvious benefit is that you build a fund of income for retirement. More importantly, these plans also permit you to defer and leverage your current income. Moreover, when you receive the proceeds from these plans in a lump sum, you may do something called "forward averaging" for everything except IRAs.

By using these plans, the government permits you to defer taxation of current income. Contributions to these plans reduce your current taxable income, and the amount you invest in these plans is not taxed now. It is taxed when the plan pays it to you.

For almost all of us, this means tax savings now and later. Most older people have smaller incomes after retirement than be-fore retirement. Older people often have more deductions for things like medical expenses. The government also allows you additional exemptions of $1,000 per person if you reach the age of 65. Under existing tax laws, the combination of lower income, more exemptions, and increased deductions means lower taxes than you would pay on current income. What is more, if you take your benefits in a lump sum, you can elect so-called "ten-year forward averaging." The effect of the election is to tax the lump sum on the spot, as if you got the money over the next ten years and had no other source of income. That is quite a tax break.

Finally, your contributions to qualified pension plans can be leveraged. You can borrow the money you want to contribute to these plans and can claim a deduction for the contributions. You get the added benefit of a deductible interest expense for the interest of the loan. Of course, leveraging only makes sense if the interest you pay on the loan (deductible or not) is less than the amount of retirement income you gain from the borrowed money.

There are three leading plans: the Individual Retirement Arrangement, known as the "IRA"; the Keogh plan; and a collection of tax-deferred annuity arrangements for state government employees, public school employees, and employees of charitable tax-exempt organizations. All three plans are pretty juicy. The rest of the significant plans are set up by incorporated employers. We will examine the major characteristics of each plan. You should see a tax or pension advisor to find out the details.

▶ **THE IRA**

The IRA has tremendous appeal, one not even dampened by the offensive advertisements for it. We get nauseated whenever we see an advertisement that proclaims "The IRA: A Tax Shelter for the Little Guy," or read misleading reports about large or effortless gains you make from IRAs. You can do well, but there are limits to your gains and you have to be disciplined.

Under current law, every taxpayer can establish an IRA and annually contribute up to $2,000 (or your annual salary, if smaller) to it. If you and your spouse both work, each of you can contribute up to $2,000. If you're in your employer's pension plan, you can still contribute up to $2,000 to an IRA and get the same tax benefits. This is a radical new change in the tax laws.

If your spouse doesn't work, you can contribute and deduct up to $250 a year to his or her own IRA. Of course, this lower limit discriminates against couples with one partner who is disabled, involuntarily laid off, or taking care of children or other dependents, but we needn't discuss that further. Take it up with your Congresspeople.

Your deductible contribution to your IRA can be made as late as the time when you file your tax return for the previous year. In other words, you can make a contribution in 1984 and report it on your tax return for 1983 as a deduction from your 1983 income, as long as you set up the IRA on or before the date you file your previous year's tax return and make the contribution before you file your return *and* you file your return by the April 15 deadline (or later if you are granted extensions).

IRAs can be constructed in many ways. Every element of the financial industry is fighting for a piece of the action. You can put your money in IRAs that invest in mutual funds, bank certificates of deposit, annuities issued by life insurance companies, stocks, or bonds. You can *not* create an IRA that invests in "collectibles," which are art objects, antiques, jewelry, stamps, baseball cards, bottle caps, comic books . . . Enough! You know what we mean.

Which is best? Who knows? Each has its problems. Annuities may overcommit you. Certificates of deposit can inflict big penalties for early withdrawal, and mutual funds can go down the tubes. Talk to the sellers of these goods. Ask *lots* of questions. They are legally obligated to answer in plain English.

Unless you invest in annuities, the tax laws compel you to give legal control of your IRA to someone else. The financial organizations that operate these plans will have you sign an agreement that makes them legal custodians or trustees of your IRA.

A word of caution. If you have heard advertisements for IRAs, you've heard the phrase "substantial penalty for early withdrawal." If, prior to age fifty-nine and a half, you terminate the plan or try to make current use of its funds in any way, you will be taxed on the distribution and subject to a penalty tax unless you are disabled. This will happen even if you leave your IRA untouched but use it as collateral to borrow money. The Service interprets *any* legal encumbrance of the IRA as a premature taxable distribution. However, if you're unhappy with the performance of your IRA, you can withdraw the money from the account and place it in another one any time you want. A word of wisdom. If you switch, do it directly from one IRA to another, not by way of yourself.

Until you reach the age fifty-nine and a half, you will always be subject to penalties for early withdrawal; there may come a time, however, when you will actually gain from a premature withdrawal. For example, if you are out of work, it may make overall tax sense to raid the IRA. Despite the penalties, the differential in your current and former tax bracket may make it relatively painless. Consequently, IRAs can be used for preretirement planning purposes other than simple balancing.

► **THE KEOGH PLAN**

Our next stop in the Land of Deferral is the Keogh plan. It's named after the Congressman who sponsored it.

In many ways, the Keogh is just a Texas-sized IRA. You can use it to defer income until you drop to a lower bracket. You may arrange to have a bank or other financial institution serve as your trustee; if you do, your plan can then invest in a variety of enterprises, and, as with an IRA, you can change accounts if you're dissatisfied with the performance of your plan.

There are two major differences between Keoghs and IRAs. The Keogh plan is designed for the self-employed person. Anyone can establish an IRA; only people who are self-employed or who have a self-employment income (and we discuss that distinction here shortly) may set up Keogh plans. The other major difference is the size of allowable annual contribution. IRA investments are limited to a maximum of $2,000 per year per taxpayer. Annual Keogh contributions can generally be up to 15% or $15,000 (whichever is smaller) of the taxpayer's annual net income from self-employment. After 1983, these limits rise to 25% or $30,000. You can therefore use a Keogh plan to defer much larger amounts of self-employment income than you can place in an IRA. If you stay below the 15%–$15,000 (or, 25%—$30,000, after 1983) ceiling, there is no limit on the number of Keogh accounts you can establish.

There are other attractive features to the Keogh plan. If you establish a plan that pays a "defined benefit" (a fixed amount of money targeted to be paid out regularly at retirement in the form of an annuity), your annual contributions may exceed $15,000 ($30,000 after 1983). The "defined benefit" plan is usually better for older people. Moreover, you can have both kinds of plans for each of your businesses. If you use both, you may enjoy higher ceilings on your deductible annual contributions.

Moreover, you don't have to be self-employed full time to set up a Keogh plan. Keogh plans may be used for *any* self-employment income. In other words, if you work full time for someone else and moonlight in some self-employed capacity, you may then contribute 15% of your moonlit 1983 income to a Keogh plan, irrespective of any pension you may have through your employer or IRA you establish with your sunlit income.

There is one drawback to the Keogh plan. If you're self-employed but you have employees who work for you, they must be covered by your Keogh plan if they have worked for you for three years or more. This can substantially increase the expense of operating your Keogh plan. Ever wonder why self-employed professionals always seem to have new receptionists? Maybe, just maybe, it has something to do with pensions.

► **TAX-SHELTERED ANNUITIES**

What the heck is an annuity? An annuity is a contract between an insurance company and the "annuitant" (the person who buys the annuity). Stripped to its essence, the contract is a wager. The insurance company bets you that you will die at or before a certain age and you bet that you will live beyond it. It is the reverse of insurance. With insurance, the company loses if you die early. With annuities, it wins if you die early. Insurance is truly a morbid business.

The annuitant is not taxed on income that he or she pays as premiums for the annuity. During that period, the insurance company invests the premiums. Once the contract begins to pay out, the annuitant is taxed gently as cash payments under the annuity are made.

Tax-sheltered annuities are the tax-deferred annuity programs for public employees, public school teachers, and employees of tax-exempt organizations such as universities, hospitals, foundations, and charities. If you're employed by one of these organizations, you can have your employer save a portion of your salary for the purchase of a tax-deferred annuity. Your employer may also choose to contribute a sum toward the annuity.

These programs are usually run by insurance companies, which like to call their products "TSAs" (tax-sheltered annuities, naturally). We call them that too.

The results of TSAs are smiliar to those of IRAs and Keogh plans. During the year in which you contribute a portion of your income to the annuity, your taxable income is reduced by the amount of your contribution, you slip into a lower tax bracket, your contribution earns income without being currently taxable, and the annuity and its income are taxed only when they are distributed to you.

These plans are very flexible. You simply sign a contract with your employer, authorizing it to channel some of your income to an insurance company. There is *no* requirement that any particular percentage of employees or class of employees participate before you can have an annuity agreement.

► **COMBINING PLANS**

One final point about all three kinds of plans for deferring income. They are not mutually exclusive. You may legally have an IRA, a Keogh plan, and an annuity plan, as long as the right kind of income goes into each account. Because you can have all three kinds of plans, the amount of income (and taxation) you may defer is the sum of the limits on your IRA, plus your Keogh plan, plus your annuity. Despite the obstacles Congress interposed between you and these devices, that can amount to a very large portion of your annual income.

For example, if you have an IRA and a Keogh plan, each year you may put away $2,000 of your salary in your IRA plus $15,000 or 15% of your self-employed income in your Keogh plan (or more, if you have a "defined benefit" arrangement). And, remember, the deductible totals will rise along with the increase in the ceiling on Keogh contributions after 1983. Again, the money you contribute may be borrowed. However, borrowing is not logical for people using annuity plans, because the contributions they make to these plans come out of their pockets in the form of reduced compensation.

A lot of prosperous people can now shield $17,000 or more from taxation each year, plus the income from that $17,000. Remember, the $17,000 ceiling ascends to $32,000 after 1983. That can lead to a substantial fund for retirement, and a greatly lowered tax bill.

Now you can go hang-gliding, but don't break anything. There's more to come.

5 DEFERRING INCOME: EMPLOYMENT CONTRACTS AND COMMERCIAL ANNUITIES

To choose time is to save time.

F. BACON

IRAs, KEOGHS, and TSAs are ways
to defer income that Congress encourages by specific, albeit grudg-
ing, legislation. There are other legal strategies for balancing your
tax rates by deferral. These strategies have to be constructed very
carefully because Congress doesn't like them. We talk about two
methods: employment contracts and commercial annuities.

These plans are very simple contractual arrangements between you and a person who, at a later date, will owe money to
you. They are variations on the installment sale. All debtors and
creditors can use them. First, we use an employer-employee relationship to demonstrate how the strategy works.

►   EMPLOYMENT CONTRACTS

You're about to go to work as a saleswoman for Fred's Storm Door
Company. This just happens to be an employment relationship
made in heaven. You have a fantastic track record in sales and
Fred has been moving his storm doors at supersonic speeds. You
can therefore expect that your commissions will be numerous and
sizable.

To keep your income in this and subsequent years relatively
smooth, you and Fred agree to deposit 50% of each commission
you expect to earn in a bank account that is automatically payable
to you when you leave the company or upon retirement. Fair is
fair, and so your deal with Fred assures some interest on the funds.
The two of you further agree that your rights to that account will
not be transferable to anyone else and that they will be forfeited if
you leave without six months' notice or if you go to work for
Ernie's All-Weather Portals, Fred's chief competitor and bitter
personal rival.

You and Fred have established a legally effective nonqualified
deferred compensation plan. Prior to the time when you become
entitled to payment of your commissions on specific sales, you and
Fred have agreed that you cannot receive the deferred portion of

the commission until one or another specific event happens. Because you established an account for the deferred portion of the commissions, you also made your rights to the account nontransferable and forfeitable. According to the tax laws, you must include these terms or you will be taxed at once. But you have devoted sufficient care to the terms of this arrangement—you will not be taxed upon the deferred payments until you receive them. You've impressed the IRS with your industry and foresightedness.

The significant key to this arrangement is that the funds are actually owed to you, but you do not have an immediate right to them. If you went to court to get immediate payment without leaving the firm or retiring, you would lose. If you went to work for Ernie and sued to get the deferred commissions, you would lose. In the eyes of the IRS agents, you cannot get the money now. They'll wait patiently until you *can*.

The other important feature is that your right to the deferred income must remain conditional for it to be placed in a special account for you. Your circumstances must change in some significant way for you to receive the money. If the events upon which your access to the account is conditioned do not take place, you may not receive the money.

In recent years, nonqualified deferred compensation plans have become very popular with high-income groups like actors, athletes, and musicians. The plans have an obvious tax advantage over employment contracts without these clauses. They spread the payment of income over many years, so that the average annual rate of tax on payments is lower than it would be if all the money were paid in a few high-income years.

Unfortunately, deferred compensation arrangements don't work as well as they once did. They were great arrangements through 1981, when the maximum tax rate on ordinary income was 70% and titanically overpaid people wanted a way to slip into lower brackets.

In 1981, Congress lowered the maximum rate to 50%. Consequently, people with very large incomes can expect to pay 50% now *and* 50% later, unless they're willing to live on very small portions of their very large incomes. Congress giveth, and Congress taketh away.

Despite these changes, deferred compensation plans are useful for people who expect to have fluctuating incomes that will affect their tax brackets. That includes almost all of us. You should have one if you expect to have a sharply *reduced* income in some later year or years. For example, a deferred compensation plan makes a lot of sense if you plan to quit working for an extended period to write the Great American Trashy Bestseller, or want to take a sabbatical. You can use the plan to shift earnings to your low-income years. The averaging of your tax rates that results will work to your advantage. Remember, also, that employers like to pay less now and more later.

Deferred compensation plans are still very useful for some people. Life insurance agents frequently use them to defer large commissions into the future and, especially, into retirement years. Likewise, they can be used to distribute a large bonus over several years to reduce its impact on taxable income.

The most important thing to remember about these plans is that they're very easy to establish. All you need is a legally enforceable agreement between the creditor and the debtor that is struck *before* the right to payment has arisen. The IRS will dismember any agreement that is struck after the creditor has a right to payment.

One more point: deferred compensation agreements are unrelated to your rights to create an IRA, Keogh Plan, or TSA. You can have all four, if you don't mind the bookkeeping and have something left to live on after you've deferred all this income.

► **COMMERCIAL ANNUITIES**

In structure, commercial annuities are just like TSAs. The only difference between the two kinds of annuities is that anyone can purchase a commercial annuity. TSAs may only be purchased by employees of the organizations we mentioned earlier.

For example, you pay $1,000 in 1981 for an annuity that will pay out $300 per year starting in 1992 and continue until you die. You survive until that date, at which time the Treasury's actuarial tables predict that you will live for ten more years. If you live only for those ten years, you will receive a total of $3,000 from the annuity contract. The Code taxes you on only $2,000 of that contract, because it deducts your $1,000 original investment from the total predicted pay-out. Therefore, ⅓ of each payment is treated as tax-free income and the remaining ⅔ is treated as part of your taxable income. Obviously, you win big if you live longer than ten years and you lose if you live less than the predicted period.

There is an attractive variant to the basic annuity contract; it's called the "variable annuity." If you buy one of these, the insurance company promises to pay an annuity that varies with the performance of the investment into which your premiums are channeled. For example, the insurance company may operate a mutual fund, into which your premiums are funneled. If the fund does well, your annuity may be whoppingly larger than it would have been if your premiums had gone into a bank account.

Of course, you can also get badly injured by a variable annuity. In the sixties and the early seventies, when the market was booming, many people bought variable annuities as a major part of their retirement plans. When the market collapsed, many annuitants who retired at the time received very limited benefits from their annuities.

The variable annuity has mutated recently into something called the "wraparound annuity." If you purchase one of these, the insurance company invests your payments for the annuity in accordance with your wishes. If the arrangements are fast and loose enough, you are simply using the annuity contract in lieu of a stock brokerage arrangement. The Congress gave them the kiss of death in 1982. They no longer work. If you are offered one, run away.

That takes care of the primary means to defer income. You can use IRAs, Keoghs, tax-sheltered annuities, deferred-compensation plans, and commercial annuities.

One of the best ways to do any or all of this is through your business. Now, we explore why you may want to blend these methods in a corporation.

CHAPTER *Six*

6 ON

BECOMING

A

CORPORATION

They cannot commit treason, nor be outlawed,
nor excommunicate, for they have no souls.
E. COKE

IF YOU'RE self-employed, or have a second income of $5,000 or more annually from business activities in addition to your regular employment, you should seriously consider the several virtues of incorporation.

We're not about to say that you should run out and incorporate. If, after reading this chapter, you feel you might want to incorporate, you should sit down with a competent tax advisor and review your situation. You will find the exercise valuable, because it could save you a great deal of money that would otherwise go directly and inexorably into the United States Treasury. In any event, the review will give you a better understanding of what you can and should do with your income.

But first, a little history. Return with us now to the fifteenth century. An up-and-coming explorer named Christopher Columbus wants to sail west to India. Unlike most of his contemporaries, he's convinced he can do it, but he's having trouble persuading investors with sufficient amounts of cash to finance this escapade. The affluent merchants of Europe are fond of their silk shirts. Understandably, they don't want to lose them to their creditors when Chris falls off the edge of the world and fails to return with his holds filled with Indian tea and spices.

After reviewing his position, Chris heads for the Spanish palace. He convinces King Ferdinand and Queen Isabella to pay for his folly. There's a lot of speculation among the palace press corps about how he convinces Isabella, but that's another story. Anyway, he also persuades the king and queen to issue a royal charter that has an important feature that encourages the other investors to sign up.

Specifically, that charter minimizes the liability of investors in the expedition. Anyone injured by the venture may hold individual investors liable only to the extent of their investment. If Amerigo Vespucci puts in 1,000 florins, he can only be held liable for 1,000 florins worth of injury that the expedition does to someone, no matter how expensive the injury.

This liability provision in the royal charter used to be a special status that only royalty could confer on investors. It has been carried forward and made available on a very democratic basis to anyone who establishes a corporation. It is the unique characteristic of corporate structure known as "limited liability" and it still means what it meant almost five hundred years ago. It sets the corporation apart from all other forms of business and is the only general form in which an investor can limit liability to the extent of his or her investment without buying insurance.

Because incorporation is so easily accomplished, many fly-by-night enterprises become corporations to take advantage of the limitation on liability. For example, virtually every taxi cab is a separate corporation these days and most of them are under-insured. The moral here is simple: it may be useful to become a corporation, but don't jaywalk.

It should not surprise you that there are limits to limited liability. If you organize a corporation but fail to operate it according to the laws that govern corporations, the courts will hold you personally liable *without limit* for any injury caused by your corporation-that-is-not-really-a-corporation.

Of course, proprietors and partners in unincorporated businesses can limit their personal liability with liability insurance. However, that kind of insurance can be very expensive.

You may think this meandering discourse on corporations is a digression, but it is not. This is a book about taxes and corpora-

SELF-INCORPORATION

tions have spectacular tax advantages. That's why we brought up the subject.

In addition to limited liability, there are several other ways in which corporations may improve your cash flow. We'll summarize those advantages and then review them in greater detail. Then we discuss why and when you should *not* incorporate.

First, corporations are taxed on their active business income at lower rates than individual taxpayers and unincorporated businesses. Second, corporations can earn passive investment income in the form of interest and dividends (especially dividends), which is subject to lower tax rates than those that apply to individual investors or unincorporated investment groups. Third, it is easier to transfer ownership interests in corporations than in other business entities. Fourth, corporations can be arranged to last forever, while partnerships and sole proprietorships live only as long as their individual owners. Fifth, corporations are easier to manage than other entities, because you can clearly delineate and restrict responsibility for different corporate decisions in ways that you can't in partnerships and sole proprietorships. Sixth, through a special provision called the "subchapter S election," newly formed corporations that initially operate at a loss can pass their losses through to their shareholders, who can use them as above-the-line deductions. Later, when the corporation begins to make a profit, it can revoke the election and become a separate low-bracket taxpayer. Finally, corporations can provide their employees with a cornucopia of fringe benefits that the corporation can deduct as expenses and the employees need not report as income. This last reason has driven many affluent people into the arms of tax planners and, thence, to incorporation.

It should be apparent that corporations are the multiply-blessed progeny of our economic system. By now you should have a vision of corporations grazing peacefully in the pastures of tax law. Before you incorporate yourself though, let's examine how these corporate characteristics operate.

When you incorporate your business, the corporation becomes the taxpayer for the corporation's income whether or not you elect subchapter S status. The tax rates on corporate profits start at a very low level. The first $25,000 in net profits is taxed at a piddling 15%. The next $25,000 will be taxed at a slightly higher rate and the peak rate, which starts at $100,000 of taxable income, will be 46%, which is four percentage points below the maximum rate on ordinary income for individual taxpayers. This rate schedule is significant, because a corporation with a modest income will almost always pay lower taxes than an individual with a comparable income.

Those tax rates apply to "earned income," the profit that flows from the business in which the corporation engages. If the corporation exists to earn passive income by investing in other corporations (or dabbles in that as a sideline), the tax rates for that activity are even more favorable. The explanation is that the tax laws permit corporations to deduct from their income 85% of the dividend income they receive from other corporations. Only 15 cents of each dollar of dividend income for the corporation is taxable to the corporation. Because the maximum corporate income tax rate is 46%, the corporation will actually be able to keep at least 93.1 cents of every dividend dollar it receives (85 cents plus 54% of 15 cents equals 93.1 cents).

Contrast this with the tax rates for individuals on dividend income. An individual taxpayer may exclude $100 of dividends from his or her income (which, by the way, is a very good reason to own stock in a high-yield mutual fund); the rest is taxed with other ordinary income at the rate that applies to the taxpayer's total ordinary income. After that $100 deduction, it's open season on dividends. The individual taxpayer will almost always pay a higher rate of tax on the amount of dividend income in excess of $100 than the corporation will pay.

Corporations are also useful containers for what would otherwise be personal stock portfolios or other assets in which people trade for short-term gains. Because small corporations are in such low tax brackets, they are fairly insensitive to differential rates of taxation on long- and short-term capital gains. You'll remember that individual taxpayers may deduct 60% of any long-term capital gain (sales of assets held for over a year). The balance is taxed as ordinary income. Because corporations can pay as much as a 28% tax on long-term gains, they are not the best place to earn income from long-term gains.

Short-term gains are a very different matter. If you purchase an asset for investment and sell it for a gain in a year or less, the income is fully taxable as ordinary income. If you're in the top bracket you can pay a tax of 50% of the income from the gain. On the other hand, corporations never pay taxes in excess of 46%, and most small corporations are in or near the 15% bracket. Consequently, corporations are the best place to earn and report short-term capital gains. But they are lousy places to take capital losses, unless they choose to be subchapter S corporations.

▶ **FRINGE BENEFITS**

Now it's time to discuss fringe benefits. There are major benefits that a corporate employer can deduct as expenses and provide to its employees, who need not report them as income. The corporation's owner may also be an employee who is eligible for these same benefits. Because a sole proprietorship or partnership cannot "employ" its owners, it can cash in on only a small fraction of this bonanza.

    1. Legal care plans.

Corporations may set up plans that provide inexpensive or free personal legal services for their employees.

CORPORATIONS GRAZING IN THE PASTURES OF TAX LAW

2. Reimbursement for educational expenses.

A corporation may pay for or reimburse its employees for education, irrespective of the subjects the employees choose to study. The subject does not have to be relevant to the corporation's business activities. Be careful here. These plans must not impermissibly discriminate among different employees, and there are other stringent standards that have to be observed. Generally, you will need quite a few employees, or else have someone else (but not your spouse or dependents) own the stock of the corporation to take advantage of this benefit.

3. Medical reimbursement plans.

Corporations may establish health care programs that pay for their employees' medical expenses. If the plan does not discriminate among employees, the corporation gets a tax deduction and each employee gets a tax-free medical benefit. Now *that* is tax shelter. This benefit is especially valuable, because individual taxpayers must itemize medical expenses and they are useful as itemized deductions only if they exceed 5% of the taxpayer's adjusted gross income. For most taxpayers, infrequent catastrophic medical expenses are the only ones that exceed that 5% deductible. Moreover, they will still be useless unless the medical expenses and other itemized deductions exceed the zero-bracket amount for your taxpayer's filing status.

On the other hand, a corporation may pay for its employees' noncatastrophic medical expenses and take a deduction for them. The employees do not personally have to bear the cost without the benefit of a corresponding deduction. The 5% limit problem is solved.

4. Disability insurance.

A corporation may buy long-term disability insurance for its employees. If an employee is disabled to the extent that he or she can't work anymore, both the corporation and the employee will receive insurance payments that compensate the corporation for loss of the employee and the employee for the loss of ability to earn income. Until payments start, the coverage is tax-free to employees. Not bad. We all may find disability insurance coming in handy.

5. Group term life insurance.

A corporation may purchase up to $50,000 worth of term life insurance for each of its working employees. The cost of the first $50,000 of insurance can be deducted by the corporation but is not taxed as income to the employees.

6. Supper money.

A corporation may pay for and deduct the cost of dinners for employees who must work late. The benefit is not taxed as income to the employee.

7. Other meals and lodging.

Corporations may pay for the meals and lodging of employees who must be in the job vicinity. This benefit is liberally construed. For example, it has been held that a ranching corporation can deduct the cost of meals and lodging provided for ranch employees who must stay out on the range to perform their duties. Here's a shocker: A rich man (we name no names) gave away his home as a museum, held by a tax-exempt corporation, while claiming a fat charitable contribution deduction. Then he lived in it, excluding the value of the meals and lodging the corporation provided him. It worked.

8. Dependent care assistance.
Corporations may establish deductible day-care plans for their employees. Once again, the plans are not treated as enriching employees. However, corporations cannot deduct more than a quarter of the cost of day-care assistance for people who directly or indirectly own more than 5% of the stock of the company.

These benefits are only available to *employees.* These fringe benefits are almost altogether unavailable to unincorporated businesses. As a rule, sole proprietors cannot employ themselves. Partners cannot employ themselves (or each other, so forget *that*). People who own unincorporated businesses or are partners in them are frozen out of these deductible fringe benefit programs. When they realize what they're missing, they usually incorporate.

The most important fact to remember is that each of these benefits reduces the taxable income of the corporation, but the benefits are tax-free to the recipients. By incorporating your business and establishing these programs, you can reduce the amount of your business income that is exposed to taxes.

There are several other significant legal benefits to incorporation. Let's review them.

▶ **LEGAL BENEFITS**

When it comes to decision-making, corporations are much less risky enterprises than partnerships. For example, all of the partners in an unincorporated business are legally bound by the decisions of any one partner. If your partner takes a dislike to you, he or she can sign limitless checks or sell the assets of the partnership, and you may have no legal remedy. If you sue your former partner, the courts may say you're bound by your partner's decision and dismiss your suit. You can only recover if you can prove that your partner's action constituted some sort of breach of duty to you. In a corporation, the officers are bound by the terms of its charter. Shareholders can sue officers who violate the terms of the charter. In any event, the shareholders' liabilities are limited to the extent of their investment in the company.

As we mentioned earlier, a properly constructed and operated corporation can last forever. The death of a corporate officer does not legally disrupt the corporation's life. In a sole proprietorship or partnership, the death of the owner or a partner can be very costly; it may even compel the closing or complete legal reorganization of the business.

Even though it is not a good place to earn long-term capital gains, the corporation can offer a very effective and legal way to create long-term capital gains out of the ordinary income it earns. Corporations may retain their earnings over a period of years. These retained earnings increase the value of the corporation, but they are often taxed at very low rates as they are earned.

The corporation can later be sold to new owners. The difference in the corporation's value from the time of incorporation to the time of the sale is taxed as a long-term capital gain, assuming that the sale is more than one year after incorporation. You can't do this in a partnership or sole proprietorship. Instead, current income is taxed to those kinds of owners at the usual rates that apply to ordinary income.

▶   **USING CORPORATIONS TO SPLIT INCOME IN THE FAMILY**

Corporations are ideal vehicles for legally splitting family income. There are infinite variations on this theme, so we can simply look at a few of the primary techniques in one example.

Mom and Pop own a hardware store. They also own the store's building and the land on which the building is located. They incorporate the store, but do not include the real estate in the assets of the corporation. Instead, they give the real estate to a trust for their minor daughter. The trust rents the real estate back to the corporation. The corporation gets a deductible rental expense and the rental income is taxed to the daughter, who is in a much lower tax bracket.

Mom and Pop may also give Daughter shares in the corporation. She is taxed on the income from the shares.

There is a maraschino cherry on this profitable arrangement. Because the corporation does not own the real estate, it has a lower book value and can be easier to sell.

Or take another tack. You may give stock to your lower-bracket children and pay them dividends. Or, you can hire them as employees and pay them salaries. Nothing prevents you from doing both.

► **THE SUBCHAPTER S CORPORATION**

The subchapter S corporation, which can pass its losses through to its shareholders, may legally do any of the things that an ordinary corporation can do. It may provide the same kinds of fringe benefits to its owners that a profitable corporation can supply to them.

The restrictions on subchapter S corporations are quite modest. The major constraints are that there cannot be over thirty-five shareholders, the corporation can't have subsidiaries, and, if it was a profitable regular (nonsubchapter S) corporation in the past, it has to limit its passive investment income.

But let's look at this with a bit more enthusiasm. Such corporations have become an especially powerful and flexible tool for income splitting, something we cover in the next chapter. The key thing to know is that, because subchapter S shareholders are taxed on the corporation's profits without regard to whether they are paid out, the people in real control of the company can pick and choose when they make actual distributions of income. Moreover, the distributions are tax-free to their recipients, because they have already been taxed.

By now it should be clear that the benefits of incorporation can be substantial. These advantages can be especially useful for people who have second incomes. A simple illustration can demonstrate this.

► **THE SMALL SERVICE CORPORATION**

Let's suppose you're a teacher who works for a public school system. In addition to your salary and company benefits, you earn about $5,000 each summer by doing some private tutoring.

You form a corporation that contracts to provide tutoring services. Your corporation will pay tax on your tutoring income at the 15% corporate rate, as opposed to the higher rates applicable to your personal income. You can reduce or eliminate the corporation's taxable income by establishing fringe benefits of the kinds described above. You can establish plans that cover your medical costs, loss of income due to disability, or create a fund for retirement. You might be especially inclined to establish a defined benefit retirement plan, because it permits larger contributions than simple IRAs or Keogh plans. Life insurance agents sell pension plans. Talk to several of them and make them compete for your business—while keeping your hand on your wallet.

If you're in a particularly aggressive mood, you could write into the corporate charter or its bylaws that you must reach into your own pocket to pay certain costs related to tutoring, such as equipment, or transportation costs you incur in working with your clients. If you do this, you may then claim a personal above-the-line deduction that will reduce your taxable personal income. Be aware, however, that the IRS is becoming more and more hostile to this expense arrangement. It is still fairly common and can be done legally, but it must be done carefully and without greed.

Your corporation may invest its income in other businesses. But you must also be certain that your corporation does not earn too much dividend or interest income. If it does, its tax return will trigger something called the "personal holding company" tax, and that can be very costly. Basically, it forces you to pay out the company's net earnings in dividends to its owners. Not good.

To get back to our example. You must also be careful that any tutoring agreement your corporation makes provides that your corporation's clients cannot compel you personally to perform the services specified in the contract. The agreement must clearly state that the corporation provides the services and provides the person who will perform them. If you don't do this, the corporation is really no more than a shell game for tax avoidance, and the IRS will make you pay for your carelessness by forcing you to pay out dividends to avoid the personal holding company tax.

Finally, some years down the line, you can sell your corporation at capital gain rates after you've piled up in it a substantial amount of retained income. That would be a fitting finale for your corporate play.

► THE PROBLEMS OF INCORPORATION

Given all these advantages, it may seem incredible that there are reasons for not incorporating. It grieves us to say this, but even corporations are imperfect.

There are legal and accounting fees that flow from the simple fact that one more legal creature has been put on our planet. Unincorporated businesses and partnerships must pay estimated taxes only on a quarterly basis. Business corporations must pay payroll taxes on a weekly, biweekly, or monthly basis. For a small business, this can create cash-flow problems.

Corporations, other than subchapter S corporations, are also subject to something called "double taxation." Corporations are taxed on their earnings and their shareholders are then taxed on corporate earnings paid out to them as dividends. This particular problem can be solved by diverting earnings into deductible fringe benefit programs for employees. As you've seen, these benefits reduce the corporation's taxable earnings without increasing the taxable income of the employees.

There are a number of other items that you must be careful about when you use a corporation for your primary or secondary income. The corporation and tax laws that regulate corporate activity are fairly complicated. You will need an advisor to attune you to them. It may be tiresome to hear this again, but we consider this a mandatory first step when you contemplate incorporation. If you take it and then play by the rules, the economic rewards can be very satisfying. By the way, the whole bill for incorporation and setting up a few fringe benefit plans should not run over $500.

7 REDISTRIBUTING INCOME IN THE FAMILY

Every day when he looked into the glass, and gave the last touch
to his consummate toilette, he offered his grateful thanks to
providence that his family was not unworthy of him.
B. DISRAELI

You MAY have believed otherwise,
but the members of your family do not have to submit to collective
taxation. They may pay taxes as individuals. If Mom and Pop and
Sis and Junior each earn income, they may each file a separate tax
return, although Mom and Pop will usually prefer to file a joint
return to get the benefit of the lower tax brackets. Nothing in the
tax law requires collective taxation of kinfolk.

This has tremendous strategic significance in tax planning. If
you can, you should fragment your family's income so that each
family member is taxed only on part of the total family income.

For example, in 1981, Pop earned $15,000, Mom earned
$15,000 and Sis and Junior had no income. They also had no
deductions. The family's taxable income was $26,000 ($30,000
minus their four $1,000 exemptions). The family's tax bill for
1981 would be $4,899.

Suppose, however, that Mom and Pop arranged to have
$6,000 of their income paid directly to their children—$3,000
each. Junior and Sis would have to file returns, but their taxable
incomes were only $2,000 ($3,000 minus a $1,000 exemption).
According to the tax tables, each has a tax liability of zero. Mom
and Pop now had a jointly taxable income of $22,000 ($24,000
minus two $1,000 exemptions) and their tax bill was $3,737. Unless our calculator has broken, the family kept $1,162 by splitting
its income that it otherwise would have had to pay in taxes. This is
a perfect example of a symbiotic relationship between high- and
low-bracket taxpayers.

The wealthier members of our society split their incomes as
regularly as tornadoes hit the lower midwest. They use such things
as permanent trusts, short-term trusts, family partnerships, and
intrafamily loans and leases. You may use them, too. All you need
is an income and a family. Most of us have those, even in these
parlous times.

Ingenious tax planners have invented innumerable ways to

take advantage of this familial option. We could easily spend several hundred pages laying them out for you. If you have the resources, you can use any combination or all of these contraptions.

There is a pitfall you must always circumnavigate carefully: the federal gift tax. For most people it won't be a major problem, but let's get it out of the way early and then we won't discuss it again when we talk about gifts.

► **THE FEDERAL GIFT TAX**

Under federal tax laws, you may give $10,000 in cash or property per year to any one person without incurring any gift tax liabilty. If you're married, you and your spouse may give up to $20,000 per year to any donee. There is no annual or lifetime limit on the total number of donees to whom you can make gifts. You can use these gift tax exclusions to make people happy and to reduce the size of your taxable estate before you return whence we all came.

The gift tax is not significant for most of us, but it will rear its head when the transactions become big. Your tax advisor should be sensitive to the application of gift tax rules to your plans for your family's income.

Now . . . on to the family! First, let's learn about lawful ways to reduce your family's taxes. We'll also discuss one fraudulent way that you should not try.

► **SUBCHAPTER S CORPORATIONS**

We've already discussed this in Chapter Six. This is just a reminder for you to consider the benefits of subchapter S corporations as instruments to split your family's income to reduce its overall tax burden.

► **TRUSTS**

Someday an aspiring film critic will earn his or her spurs with a canny essay on the role of trust funds in screwball comedies. Trusts have an honorable role in those movies. It's a safe bet that half of them have at least one dizzy ingenue who is heiress to some enormous trust managed by nasty old codgers. You could also bet the farm that the fund will be used at the end of the movie to save lovable and zany characters from some terrible fate that would otherwise befall them.

Well, you can use trusts to save you from the Tax Man. The tax laws make trusts very attractive instruments for protection of your income. First, you're about to master some very simple terminology.

A trust is an arrangement in which one person, called the "grantor," transfers the legal rights of ownership of property to someone else, called the "trustee." The grantor and trustee can be the same person. That should begin to suggest part of what can happen here. The property is held and managed by the trustee for the benefit of a third person, who is called the "beneficiary." The fate of the property is fixed according to the grantor's plans, which get locked in concrete when the trust is set up.

The property that goes into the trust is called the "corpus," the "res," or the "principal." The income from the trust is called the "income." (Some things never change.)

Trustees must be very careful people. The law of trusts holds them to very high standards of conduct in managing trusts. These are referred to as their "fiduciary obligations." If trustees carry out their duties in a dishonest, reckless, or negligent manner, their beneficiaries can sue the heck out of all of them. The courts are very tough on trustees. It doesn't take much evidence to prove a breach of fiduciary obligations.

Trusts are generally used for two purposes. First, they allow grantors to shift income-producing property out of their hands, where it would be taxed at painful rates, into those of beneficiaries in lower tax brackets. Second, they can be arranged to control the flow of income to the beneficiary. This is done for two reasons: to create a reasonably predictable amount of liability for all of the participants and to prevent the beneficiary from spending the corpus at rates of speed that the grantor believes are unacceptable.

For a trust to be effective for tax purposes, the grantor must truly give up ownership of the corpus; otherwise, the grantor will be taxed on the income from the corpus. If the grantor has really transferred ownership and control of the corpus to the trust, neither the grantor nor the trust will be taxed on income from the corpus that the trust pays to its beneficiaries; instead, over the long run, the beneficiaries pay the taxes on their trust income.

The trust itself is not taxed, except on income that it does not distribute to its beneficiaries; even so, the rate of taxation on income kept by the trust may be lower than the rate applicable to the beneficiary's income. In cases like that, trusts can be used to accumulate income in relatively low tax brackets for eventual distribution to beneficiaries.

The tax laws try to attack this delayed payment of accumulated income by imposition of a special penalty under provisions called the "throw-back" rules. The penalty can be completely avoided if the trust can pass through a gigantic loophole in the throw-back rules; no penalty is imposed if the trust is completely terminated by payment of the principal and its accumulated income to the beneficiaries before or when they reach the age of twenty-one. This loophole may be the source of the standard line, "I'll be coming into some money when I turn twenty-one."

With these rules in mind, let's look at the basic forms of trusts. There are two: the permanent trust and the short-term trust.

▶ **PERMANENT TRUSTS**

The permanent trust is relatively useless for our purposes, so we'll dispose of it as quickly as possible. Usually, it is set up to last through as many generations as the laws that govern these things permit. In effect, it is a kind of permanent bank account managed by very cautious professional trustees, who are directed by the trust agreement to hand out just enough income to keep the beneficiaries in the modest (or appalling) style to which the grantor wants them accustomed. The balance of the income accumulates in the trust and some portion is paid to the trustees as a management fee.

These trusts aren't useful for people of modest means. Because they are irrevocable, most of us can set up permanent trusts only by parting company with everything we own. We might be able to do that for a little while, but almost all of us wouldn't want to give everything away for good. That is very painful.

▶ **SHORT-TERM TRUSTS**

The short-term trust is a much tastier—and extremely popular—planning instrument. It usually takes one of two basic forms. It's usually used to support older family members or to pay for children's higher education.

There is one pitfall that must be scrupulously avoided in the management of any trust. The trust should not be used to satisfy a grantor's legal obligation to "support" a beneficiary, except when the grantor suffers extreme financial distress. If it is used to "support" a beneficiary, the income from the trust is taxed as the grantor's income, and that, in turn, defeats the purpose of constructing the trust.

There is no single definition of "support." The federal government has its own foggy definition, but each state may add its definition to the rules, and those definitions vary considerably from state to state. Your lawyer or trustee should assure you that he or she is aware of the relevant rules and construct your trust accordingly.

► **SHORT-TERM TRUSTS FOR SENIORS**

Let's turn our attention first to a common form of the trust for older adults. The grantor is usually a son or daughter who has prospered. The grantor transfers assets to a trust designed to last for the lifetime of his or her parents. The son or daughter may lawfully act as trustee; doing this will reduce administrative expenses.

As long as the parents live, the income from the trust will be paid to the parent-beneficiaries. The beneficiaries are the only persons taxed on the income they receive from the trust (unless the trust retains some earnings or the trustees take a taxable management fee). When the beneficiaries die, the corpus returns ("reverts") to the children.

For a very simple reason, this arrangement reduces the grantor's tax liability and increases the amount of money available for transfer to the beneficiary. If there is no trust, the children will be taxed on their entire income, including that portion which they intend to give to their parents. The children are in a higher bracket than their parents (otherwise, there's no point in doing this) and would pay more tax on the income they intend to transfer to the parents, which will leave less to transfer than if the parents receive the income directly from a trust. If the children who are in higher tax brackets than their parents do not use trusts, the money they give will be reduced by income taxation *and,* if they are stunningly generous, gift taxation. Generally, gift taxes are never levied on the middle class; we ignore them. If the assets are placed in a trust, the income is taxed only once and at the lower rate that applies to the parent's income. Let's look at an example.

Every year, Junior and Sis each give Pop $3,000 for support. Pop is 75. Junior and Sis are in the 40% bracket. Therefore, Junior and Sis must earn $10,000 to have $6,000 left to give Pop. If they have enough income-producing assets, the better solution for Junior and Sis is to set up a trust for Pop that pays him approximately $6,700 each year. Pop will pay about 10% of that in tax and wind up with about as much as he had without the trust. Junior and Sis do much better with a trust because there is no tax burden for them that compels them to make more to give the same $6,000. When Pop dies, they will get back the assets producing the trust's income without assuming any tax liability on the returned assets. Income produced by gains from the sales of the assets generally becomes taxable to Junior and Sis. In case you did not know it, trusts like this are set up every day. Furthermore, they do not reduce retired peoples' rights to Social Security benefits.

Junior and Sis must remember to construct the trust in light of federal and state rules about support obligations. If Junior and Sis support Pop with this trust and under state law they have a direct obligation to support him, Junior and Sis may have to pay income taxes on the income from the trust that is used to discharge their support obligation. There is a fairly large but rather harsh loophole here; the IRS takes the position that it will not tax the grantor-children in states where the parents are obliged to exhaust their own resources before turning to their children. It is harsh because it compels the elderly to strip themselves of any income or emotional security they may derive from their own assets before they can demand help from their children.

► **SHORT-TERM TRUSTS FOR THE YOUNG**

Another powerful planning device involves establishing short-term trusts for minors. "Short-term" is a bit of a misnomer here, because the trust must exist for at least ten years to gain the full benefits of the applicable tax rules. By the way, any object of your bounty, except your spouse, can qualify. Kids are just the most common example.

The arrangement commonly works along these lines. Let's suppose the parents transfer $5,000 a year for five years to a trust for the benefit of their two very young children. The annual income from the trust is shifted into "custodial accounts" (these have other tax benefits and we've defined them for you a few pages further on) that are established for the benefit of the children at a bank.

Under most state laws, minors are not entitled to the money in the accounts until they reach the magic age of twenty-one. When the children begin college, trust income in the bank accounts (and whatever income earned by the trusts not yet moved to the custodial bank accounts) may be turned over to the kids and used to pay for tuition.

If the parents want to avoid being taxed on the trust income, it must be used to pay for things that are not necessities. College tuition is the primary example of a "non-necessary" expenditure. If the income is used to pay for room and board at a prep school, Mom and Pop will be taxed, because room and board constitute "support" under state law.

The relevant definition of support varies from state to state. Generally, you can avoid taxation from application of the support rule by using trust monies to pay for luxuries, rather than necessities, before the children are twenty-one.

Meals, lodging, medical payments and so on are usually defined as necessities. If trust income is used to pay for them, the grantor will be taxed on the income used to foot these bills.

Luxuries include such items as trips to Europe and college tuition. No state court or legislature that we know of has created a rule that treats either as a necessity. So far, no state has ever required a parent to send a child to college or to pay his or her way to Katmandu. The point is, if there is doubt in your mind about what constitutes a necessity, check it out before using trust funds to pay the bills for it.

When the children turn twenty-one, or some other age chosen by the parents, the trust principal can be returned to the parents. The trick here is to make sure that the principal has been firmly stuck in the trust for at least ten years. That ensures that the trust income will be taxed to the lower-bracket child or trust and not to the higher-bracket parents.

This area can be a bit treacherous. The date that the trust was established does not absolutely protect the grantors from personal taxation on the trust's income. The true test is when the *principal* was placed in the trust.

For example, let's suppose that part of the principal is placed in a trust when the child is seven and another part when the child is ten. If the trust principal is transferred back to the parents when the child is nineteen, the income from the first part placed in the trust is not taxed to the grantors. It has been in trust for ten years. However, the second part has been in the trust for only nine years. The parents *will* be taxed on income that can be attributed to that second portion of the principal. Obviously, the parents must make sure that each portion of the principal is in the trust for ten years. Otherwise, the Tax Man Cometh.

One happy feature of these trusts is that the parents can be the trustees. You don't need a lot of technical expertise to manage one of these trusts, and the tax return for trusts are relatively easy to prepare, especially if the trust is a very simple one. There are no reasons (other than laziness) to pay management or accounting fees. Furthermore, the assets placed in trust can be of limitless variety (though it's not a good idea to use contraband).

If the trust is properly constructed, the grantors may have access to the principal as long as the trust exists. If the trust document permits it, the grantors may borrow back from the trust some or all of the principal. In turn, the grantors pay interest to the trust on the loan and deduct that interest from their income. When the trust terminates, the parents-grantors-trustees can engage in a kind of Chinese Fire Drill with the principal. First, the parents can write a check to the trustees (themselves) to repay the loan. Second, the trustees then write a check on the trust account back to the parents for the amount of the principal in the trust. In effect, the parents have retained the use of the principal while it was technically in trust and paid for the children's education in the form of deductible interest expenses.

You have to control your greed if you're going to try this. Wait a good long while before you borrow the principal from the trust. If it is done properly, you get classical symbiotic shifting. You get an interest deduction from the low-bracket trust and move interest income into it. The IRS may challenge this transaction, but it will lose, especially when the borrowing takes place long after the trust has been established.

You should have a lawyer set up the trusts. Don't pay a lot of money. Any banker will help to set up custodial accounts. Don't let his drool get your cuffs soggy.

Remember: the trustees (i.e., probably yourselves) must prudently manage the trust's assets. If they are managed sloppily or earn less than they could reasonably be expected to earn, the children may sue the trustees and have a good chance of winning.

▶ **A BOGUS TRUST THAT YOU SHOULD AVOID LIKE THE PLAGUE: THE FAMILY TRUST**

Now, you may not believe this, but there are greedy brigands who aren't satisfied with lawful strategies to keep your family's income from becoming income tax. These bounders advise taxpayers to follow fraudulent familial paths to tax reduction.

We particularly have one such dangerous avenue in mind. It's a phony tax shelter called the "family estate trust." It doesn't work, the courts don't recognize it as lawful, and it will put you into a boiling pot of Audit Soup. Nevertheless, the family estate trust is used by large numbers of Americans.

Proponents of this shell game will advise you to create a sack-like trust large enough to hold all of your assets and income. In effect, you and the rest of your family sign over to the trust all of your income from services, including salary, or some combination of salary plus other income. The trust then distributes the money as it is needed to family members.

This is nothing short of simple fraud. There is absolutely no doubt in our minds that these trusts are impermissible under current law. The Code, the apparatchiks at the Service, and the tax courts clearly agree that you cannot assign to a trust income from personal services—which includes salary, tips, and professional fees.

It is depressing (yet somehow oddly inspiring, like the be-

AUDIT SOUP

havior of lemmings) to report that people try this anyway, all the time. And, in court, they always lose.

Avoid the family estate trust. You probably won't go to jail if you try it, but it won't work, you've effectively stapled a "Please Audit Me" sign on your tax return, and you will pay hefty penalties for your folly. We now leave this seamy vein and get back to the legitimate stuff.

► **CUSTODIANSHIPS**

These arrangements are less ambitious variations on the trust theme. Basically, a custodianship is an arrangement in which one person (the "transferor") transfers money to a bank, savings and loan association, credit union, or stock-trading account permitted by state law. The official title of the account is something like "Account of Peter Parent, As Custodian for the Benefit of Charles Child." The money in the account, and the income from it, belong to Charles Child, but the custodian has legal control of it. The child is entitled to the annual income from the account, although most children are kept in the dark about this feature of the deal. The principal and any undistributed income must be paid to the child when the child reaches the age of majority as defined by state law.

These arrangements are simple to establish. Unfortunately, they have fewer advantages than trusts.

One drawback is that the principal does not go back to the transferor. If you establish a custodial account, you must be prepared to part with the principal permanently. For a lot of people, this means that smaller sums will be used in custodial accounts than in short-term trusts.

The pay-out age also varies from state to state. The custodial arrangement is bound by the definition of majority in the state where the account is established. That varies from sixteen to twenty-one.

Each child for whom you want to establish a custodial account must have a separate one. Joint custodial accounts cannot be established for two or more children. One account per child is really a good thing. The bank does not mind and it keeps things tidy.

Unlike trusts, there are also limitations on the kinds of property that can be placed in custody. Land, copyrights and other "intellectual properties," and tangible personal property such as paintings, jewelry, or cars cannot be placed in custodial accounts.

Despite these limitations, custodial accounts have value. They are cheap and easy to establish, and they relieve the transferor of liability for income from the custodial assets. They are commonly used as parking lots to hold income from short-term trusts for children until they reach adulthood.

► **INTRAFAMILY LOANS**

This strategy is rapidly gaining popularity, which probably means the IRS will reinforce its so far almost completely unsuccessful attack on it.

Warning: this is a very hot legal topic. The United States Supreme Court may decide to review one of these situations in the future. If so, there is a good chance that the strategy will be declared legally defective. As things stand, there are two basic ways to use loans to reduce tax liability in the family.

The first way is the low-interest or no-interest loan. The background idea here is that a relatively wealthy family member decides to make a gift to a family member in a lower income bracket. Instead of making an outright gift, which has limited tax benefits and means really parting with wealth, the generous soul "loans" the money to the worthy but less fortunate family member and charges little or no interest on the loan. Consequently, the money is not taxed to the lender as a gift or as income to the recipient. The recipient pays no tax on the loan. Of course, if the recipient invests the loan, he or she will be taxed on the income from the investment, unless it is invested in a tax-free activity.

Typically, these loans are structured as payable "on demand," so that the lender can insist on repayment at will. Partly, this is done to prevent the IRS from interpreting the loan as the gift it really is and imposing a gift tax on it. This is not an important strategy for small-gift givers, because the gift tax is only imposed on fairly large gifts. We need not discuss this in more detail, because if your gifts are large enough to interest the IRS, you can afford a flock of tax lawyers and accountants to protect and advise you.

These loans produce perfect income splitting. The "borrower" invests the money and makes money, the "lender's" taxes are reduced, and the lender is still fat and sassy, knowing he or she can demand the money back any time. You win, and the IRS loses.

The reverse of the low-interest or no-interest loan is the excessive-interest loan. The parties are reversed here. The poorer relation lends money at an astronomical rate of interest to the wealthier family member. The rich relation then claims an interest deduction for interest payments on the loan. The poor relative pays tax on the interest income, but at a lower rate than the rate at which the rich relative deducts them. If it weren't for this arrangement, the upper-bracket relative would simply pay his or her taxes at the high rates without the benefit of the interest deduction. This tactic produces symbiotic taxation. Income is shifted to the low-bracket relative and the high-bracket relative gets an honest deduction.

You might get the best of both worlds through a two-step transaction. The high-bracket relative *could* lend money at a very low rate of interest to the low-bracket relative, who could then lend it back to the high-bracket relative at a crushing rate of interest. This is theoretically possible, but it is very risky. If you try something like this, you are begging for an IRS audit.

If you're crazy enough to try it, you ought to separate the two steps by a long period of time, so that they really aren't the same transaction. Furthermore, if one of the relatives in this scheme is a minor, you ought to have an independent trustee appointed to represent the child's interests.

▶ **INTRAFAMILY LEASES**

In form, these arrangements are very similar to intrafamily loans. They are typically used to shift rental income from high-income professional people to their minor children. Our explanation takes the form of an example.

Poppa Doc, a successful brain surgeon, owns his own office building in which he rents space to doctors and medical malpractice lawyers (defense only, please). Over the years, he has completely depreciated the building, so the building is useless as a tax shelter. From a tax standpoint, it's no longer worthwhile for him to take the income from the building.

After consulting his tax lawyer, Poppa Doc creates a trust for the benefit of his minor children, Sis and Junior, and gives his office building to the trust. The trust then leases the building back to Poppa Doc.

Poppa Doc can now claim a rental expense deduction for his payments to the trust. He can use that deduction to reduce his taxable income. In this transaction, the landlord becomes the tenant and the tenants become subtenants.

If the trust is constructed to distribute income as it is earned,

Junior and Sis report the rental income on their individual returns. If the trust is arranged to keep the profits but to terminate and pay out at a specific date, the trust pays income taxes until then and the after-tax income is retained for eventual distribution to Sis and Junior.

This arrangement can be used for any kind of business property. In addition to real estate, it can be used for equipment. Think about this the next time you climb into your dentist's chair. You may be sitting in a part of a trust.

Of course, Poppa Doc may not want to part permanently with his building. In that case, his tax lawyer should advise him to establish a "short-term" (i.e., ten-year or longer) trust, with a provision that the property comes back to him after ten years. The IRS is not wild about these leaseback–short-term trusts, but the courts seem to respect them at present, if they are constructed to observe all the legal formalities: an independent trustee, a complete outright transfer for at least ten years, and a genuine leasing agreement that truly binds the parties. Have your trust built by someone who knows how to do it correctly.

There's an additional dimension to this strategy. It turns on whether Poppa Doc gives or sells the property to the trust.

If Poppa Doc makes a gift of the building to the trust, the depreciated value of the building does not change. If, for example, Doc's depreciated the building's value to 40% of its original value, the trust gets to continue to offset the rental income by depreciating the value of the building from that 40% base to zero. If Doc has already depreciated the building to zero, the trust cannot depreciate it further.

If Doc *sells* the building to the trust, the Depreciation Dance can begin again at 100% of the price of the building to the trust. That helps if the beneficiaries of the trust are in fairly high brackets.

You can do this with a short-term trust, too, but there are additional steps in the Dance: (1) transfer cash to the trust; (2) the trust buys the property; (3) the property is depreciated; (4) when the trust terminates, it transfers the building back to the grantor.

▶ **JOINT OWNERSHIP OF PROPERTY**

Joint ownership is yet another means to split income. It also can be used to reduce the cost of probating an estate.

Because we're concerned here with income tax rather than

real estate and gift taxes, we give short shrift to gift and estate tax issues. In most cases, the income tax liability is clearer and much more significant.

Joint ownership arrangements are somewhat complicated. The property laws that govern them vary from state to state. There's a further layer of complexity in states that treat marital property as community property (California and Louisiana are among them).

There are three basic types of joint ownership: "tenancies in common," "joint tenancies with rights of survivorships," and "tenancies by the entirety." Each is significantly different from the other two.

A tenancy in common has three key characteristics. Each "tenant" owns an individual share of the property. Any tenant can sell his or her share in the property. When a tenant dies, that tenant's individual interest in the property becomes part of his or her estate.

A joint tenancy with the right of survivorship differs from a tenancy in common in only one important aspect. If a tenant dies, his or her share automatically passes to the surviving tenants. A tenancy by the entirety is basically a joint tenancy between a husband and wife, with right of survivorship.

Joint tenancies and tenancies by the entirety can be used to reduce the cost of probating an estate. The right of survivorship causes ownership of the property to pass to the survivors(s) when one joint tenant dies. Probate courts don't have to order or supervise the transfer.

This is a basic premise of the "How to Avoid Probate" school of legal literature. Put everything in joint tenancy, and all you have to do is pay taxes on the total value of the dear departed's share of the jointly owned property. This method works beautifully to avoid probate, but it contains some risks.

The reward of survivorship can encourage a joint tenant to hasten a fellow tenant's demise. This is unlikely, but it has happened outside Perry Mason novels.

A more serious and ordinary problem is that the creation of a joint tenancy is an irreversible transaction. Once you make someone a joint tenant, you can't unilaterally change the legal arrangement. Your fellow tenant has rights in the property that are completely equal to yours. If you have a falling out (or a divorce), the right of survivorship and the other rights of ownership generally remain unaffected. Oh, you can go to court and get the property divided, but that can reduce the value of the property or render it worthless. How do you divide a jointly owned home or a Van Gogh? You can only do it if one partner buys out the other. If neither can afford that, the joint tenants remain stuck with each other. This produces a lovely situation where the tenants grimly sit it out, each waiting for the other to shuffle off the mortal coil.

In other words, joint ownership is great if the tenants get along. If they don't, then they spend their twilight years perusing the obit column and cursing the persons who advised them to put their property in joint tenancy.

The situation can be aggravated, since each joint tenant has a right to sell his or her share to someone else. A disgruntled joint tenant can unilaterally impose a new tenant on the old ones. Generally, this can't happen in tenancies by the entirety because it requires consent of both spouses. In other relationships, this can be explosive.

Income taxation of jointly owned property is fairly simple. The several kinds of joint ownership are taxed differently.

Tenants in common are taxed on each tenant's proportional share in the property. For example, if each tenant had a one-half interest in a share of stock that paid $1,000 in annual dividends, each tenant would report $500 of income from the share.

Joint tenants are taxed somewhat differently. Each tenant is taxed on his or her proportional share of the *net* income from the property. The proportional share is determined by state law. If one tenant pays for a deductible real estate tax or interest expense of the property (real estate taxes or interest, for example), he or she may generally deduct the payment in full.

Suppose you own a one-half joint interest in an apartment building but you pay all of the expenses on the building. You may reduce your taxable share of the net income by the taxes and interest you pay. Your fellow tenant is not so lucky; he or she will pay taxes on 100% of his or her share of the net income.

Otherwise, joint tenants bear equal shares of the freight. Gains and losses on sales and exchanges of jointly owned property are allocated equally to each tenant.

With one exception, all jointly owned property is taxed according to this scheme. The tax laws exempt U.S. Series E and EE Savings Bonds from this treatment. Tax liability for interest is allocated in proportion to the actual contribution of joint tenants for the purchase of the bonds. This ostensibly encourages parents to buy them for their children and hold them for them. At maturity, the child gets the bond but has paid no tax on its income.

To sum it all up, joint ownership can have beneficial effects on your stream of income and taxes. It can reduce income, gift, and estate taxes (a rich person's problem we are not concerned with) and reduce or eliminate the costs of probate. Joint owner- ships are cheaper to establish than trusts.

Joint ownership can also be used to establish symbiotic rela- tionships with low-bracket taxpayers. For example, Pop might purchase a condominium in joint tenancy with his daughter. If she can make the mortgage payments but can't afford the interest, Pop can pay all the interest on the mortgage and deduct it. Varia- tions on this theme are discussed in our chapter on real estate.

All in all, joint ownership can be a very efficient way to hold indivisible assets, such as real estate that you want to keep in the family. The tenancy in common is the cleanest and simplest form but lacks the survivorship feature that removes the property from probate.

On the other hand, joint ownership arrangements can require consideration of complex and interlocking questions about taxa- tion and management of the jointly owned assets. In any form, it can stimulate feuding among the joint owners. They may disagree about management and retention of the asset. Individually, they can replace themselves with other equally bumptious successors.

Carefully consider all of this before using joint ownership to reduce your taxes and other legal bills. Your fellow tenants may be boon companions or may become the bane of your existence.

► **GIFTS**

Although it's not a very useful strategy, you *can* reduce your in- come taxes by giving gifts to family members (or anyone else, for that matter). The classic time to do it is when you own an asset that has dramatically increased in value and you want to sell it, but you also want to avoid excessive taxation on the income.

It can work this way. Suppose you want to make a gift to your son who is in the 20% bracket. Twenty-five years ago, you pur- chased 100 shares of Fred's Storm Door Company for a dollar a share. We all know how well Fred's stock did. Your shares are now worth $3,000.

You did equally well; you're now in the 50% bracket. If you sell the stock yourself, you will have a capital gain of $2,900, on which you will pay a tax of $580 (50% of 40% of $2,900). That means only $2,420 will be left to give to your son. Instead, you make a gift of the stock to him. On your advice, he sells the stock and realizes an after-tax gift of $2,768. Transferring the stock *before* selling it increased the after-tax gift by $348.

There is one thing you should *not* do in this kind of transaction. Do not arrange the sale of the asset *before* giving it away. If you do this, the IRS will treat the gift as a sham constructed to avoid taxes. If you ignore this warning, *you,* not your son, will be taxed on the sale of the stock, and at the rates that apply to your income bracket, not his.

With apologies to Gertrude Stein, a gift must be a gift must be a gift. Your son must be free to do with the gift as he pleases. He may be too stupid, pig-headed, or greedy to take your advice to sell the stock at the top of the market, but the IRS doesn't approve of this kind of package deal. You can't give your son the stock with an attached sale. In the eyes of the Service, you're really giving him the proceeds of your sale of the stock.

▶ **FAMILY EMPLOYMENT**

You don't have to make your kid a partner in your business to use your family to shield your income from taxation. There is nothing that prevents you from hiring family members to work for your business.

This is not an unlimited gift. You can't hire your son to mow your lawn and deduct his pay from your taxable income, because that is not a business expense. On the other hand, you can employ him in your gardening business to mow someone else's lawn and take a deduction for his salary and benefits. Moreover, in most cases you don't have to pay Social Security on the income of minors employed in your family business. By the way, if the child does very well, he or she can then set up an IRA and pack away up to 2,000 tax-free dollars of those earnings every year. Believe it or not, it is done.

▶ **FAMILY PARTNERSHIPS**

You can take the next step and make your offspring partners in your business. This is another very common and acceptable way to split family income.

The basic idea is very simple. You convert your business from a sole proprietorship to a family partnership. The result is equally straightforward. In place of one owner taxed on all the income of the business, you substitute two or more partners, each of whom are taxed on a portion of the business income. At least one of the partners ought to be in a much lower income bracket, which then works to reduce the overall tax liability for the business and its operators.

As you should expect by now, you must follow certain rules if you want the IRS to respect the arrangement. It must be constructed so that it is a legally genuine partnership. Only certain kinds of family partnerships can have these tax benefits.

First, and most important, in order to be successful, the partnership interest must be real. To prevent a successful attack by the IRS you should first do the following:

1. Have the partnership agreement in writing.
2. Make sure the partnership interests are lawfully distributed among the partners in accordance with the terms of the partnership agreement.
3. Tell the people you do business with that you have partners.
4. Annually file a Partnership Information Tax Return (Form 1065).
5. Act as if it is a partnership. Believe it and it will be true. If you don't, it will turn to dust, or worse, an audit.

By creating a partnership, a portion of the profits from the business is added to the income of the new partners. Each partner is then taxed only on his or her share of the income from the partnership. Although you must file Form 1065 yearly, the partnership itself is not taxed; only the partners pay taxes.

This is an important thing to remember. Partnership profits are always *taxed*, even if they are retained as partnership assets and are not actually distributed to the partners. This is different from the corporate arrangement. The corporation is taxed on its profits, but its employees and officers are not taxed on corporate income that the corporation retains. Partnerships are not directly taxed, but the partners are *always* liable for any profits, even those that are retained in partnership accounts.

Converting the family business into a partnership only has tax value when you add partners in lower tax brackets. Otherwise you're wasting your time and profits. Consequently, the best partners are relatives, parents, children, or your siblings who have not yet reached or have already passed their peak earning years. There is no tax advantage to adding your spouse as a partner; the two of you undoubtedly already split your income by filing a joint return.

The tax laws limit the kinds of partnerships that can be used to split income with your family. In the words of the Code, to be eligible for the tax benefits of a family partnership, the partnership must be one in which capital is "a material income-producing factor." This could be a business with substantial product inventories or capital, such as business equipment. The duration of the partnership is not significant. You can also have a family partnership for short-term activities like developing a piece of land.

It is clear that you cannot create a family partnership out of a service business unless the other family members also really provide the services. Examples of ineligible service businesses might be your work as a lawyer, accountant, architect, or doctor. A minor child can't provide these services, so how could he or she be a genuine partner? If you don't have a genuine partner, you don't have a genuine partnership.

There are several ways to make family members partners. It's easy if the partners are adults. You just draw up a written partnership contract between you and your partner. If you want to make a mature minor a partner, the tax laws will generally respect the child's status as a genuine partner to such an agreement if he or she is competent. This means the child is considered to be able to manage his or her affairs properly, that is, more or less like an adult.

The big tax advantage comes from making immature minor children partners in a business (assuming capital is a major factor), because they will probably be in the lowest possible tax brackets. The most sensible way to accomplish this is to create a trust for the child and give the trust a partnership share. The trust must be drafted so that the income is not taxed to you as grantor or to your estate when you die. To be legally effective, the trust must have several features:

1. It must be irrevocable.
2. You must not have power to amend it.
3. You must not retain the power to shift principal or income of the trust.
4. The trust must continue to exist if you die.
5. You must have no power over the distribution or retention of the trust's income.
6. You must not have a fixed right to borrow any portion of the trust's income or principal—except at a very well-structured distance.

7. You should not be the trustee. Pick a capable friend, neighbor, or maybe a tax advisor.

It should be apparent that this may constitute a major change in the way you do business. You should consider it carefully before you make it. You are almost irreversibly altering the nature of your affairs. To change the arrangement probably requires dissolution of the partnership and complete reorganization of the business.

There are several other limitations on the arrangement. The most significant one is that the person or persons who actually do the work of the partnership must receive a reasonable salary before any profits can be allocated to the inactive partners. Second, your profit-sharing percentage, on the basis of comparative dollars invested, cannot be smaller than that of the partner(s) you add for tax purposes. This isn't unreasonable; it's a means to keep family partnerships from being shams.

Let's look at a brief example that combines the use of a trust and family partnership. Pop owns a small hardware store. To reduce his tax burden, he establishes a trust for his son Junior and puts funds in it. The trustee is Sam, Pop's neighbor, best friend, and a capable businessman. Pop has a very successful store and after carefully inspecting the business and its books, Sam concludes that Junior's trust should buy a profit-sharing percentage in the store. On behalf of Junior, the trust purchases a partnership interest in the store equal to ½ of the business and receives a profit-sharing percentage. Pop continues to manage the store and receives a salary for his work. After paying bills, including a reasonable salary for Pop, he and the trust then each receive 50% of the net profits. The trustee deposits Junior's share of the profits in a custodial account for Junior's benefit.

The advantages of family partnerships should be clear. You can split income with needier family members and get them involved in the operation of the family business. The IRS encourages you to reach these goals by allowing you to reduce your income- and estate-tax liability. (PS: The trust could be a short-term trust. The IRS doesn't like this, although the government is on pretty weak legal ground.)

The disadvantages should be equally clear. First, you must give up some of the rights of ownership and control over your business's form. Second, in all partnerships, each partner has the right to participate, directly or indirectly, in decisions about the operation of the partnership or transfer of their interests. That means

Pop's friend Sam may butt in a bit too often. Finally, partners have a claim on the assets of the partnership if they decide to withdraw from it or it is liquidated.

On a simple numerical basis, the disadvantages outnumber the advantages. Nevertheless, the tax advantages often make the risks attractive to everyone but the Treasury.

By the way, nothing prevents you from using the corporate form to split family income. You might even decide to use the subchapter S form. People do it all the time, and it is a powerful

CONVERTING YOUR HOME INTO A COTTAGE INDUSTRY

technique because it causes child-shareholders to be taxed on income that the corporation does not actually pay out. Sit down with your advisor and work it out.

Well, that takes care of the family. You've successfully converted your hearth and home into a thriving cottage industry that works around the clock to reduce your taxes. Home sweet home! Which brings to mind our next topic, real estate.

CHAPTER *Eight*

▶ 8 | REAL

ESTATE

INVESTMENT

Hame's hame, be it ever so hamely.
J. ARBUTHNOT

IN THIS CHAPTER, we talk about
the benefits and burdens of three basic types of real estate investment:

1. Home ownership.
2. Ownership of commercial real estate on some profit-making
   basis.
3. Ownership of "hybrid" real estate, which serves as your home
   and as commercial real estate.

Each form may have tremendous advantages for you, but that
depends on two things: your "personal economic circumstances,"
which translates into the amount of money you have available to
invest in real estate; and your tax situation, which means the tax
savings and liabilities you incur as a result of real estate investments.

A word of advice. This topic is a bit complicated. To ease the
pain, we suggest you read the material about each of the three
major types of real estate at different times.

► **HOME OWNERSHIP**

For most of us, a home is the only kind of real estate we will ever
own. As you know, in recent years that particular goal has receded
for many people. The costs of new construction or renovation of
older housing and the cost of loans for mortgages have increased
steadily and painfully in the last few years.

It's a pretty depressing subject right now and has turned into
fodder for demagogues at all points of the political compass. Every
so often, governments and lending institutions establish some new
scheme to reverse this trend. So far, such schemes seem to work
too well (in which case, the funds used to power them are ex-
hausted quickly and things drift back toward disaster) or they
don't work at all.

► **THE BENEFITS OF HOME OWNERSHIP**

There are several valuable benefits attached to home ownership, not the least of which is dispensing with oppressive landlords. You become your own master and (if you're that sort of person) can get drunk on the power to call a plumber anytime you're ready to fall more deeply into debt.

The other benefits are only slightly less spectacular. For one thing, the government does not tax you on the value of occupying your own property. It could, but electoral suicide is not looked on with much favor in Congress. Instead, the Code classifies this enjoyment as "imputed income." It is potentially taxable, but actually free from taxation. For reasons of public policy (or, if you prefer, to keep home ownership attractive), Congress acknowledges that this satisfaction could be taxed but it refrains, largely because the social aggravation (and the arithmetic) would be too complex. If it were not for this rule, the other benefits of home ownership would diminish or completely disappear. Still, the fact is home ownership is a way to earn tax-free income.

The other tax benefits come in the form of itemized deductions for state and local taxes and interest on your mortgage and home improvement loans. If you use your home exclusively as a home and use no part of it for business of any sort (such as renting any portion of it to someone), the deductions are itemized below the line on Schedule A of your Form 1040. This means home ownership is a way to claim current deductions for generating nontaxable imputed income. That's a good example of conversion.

The other major benefit is somewhat intangible but can count for something—and, sometimes, for quite a lot. It is a historical fact that real estate generally and steadily increases in value over a time at a rate greater than that of inflation. For this reason, it is considered a good investment.

This rate of appreciation varies in different years, for different kinds of real estate, and in different locations. In the early seventies, real estate rapidly appreciated in all parts of the United States.

More recently, the rate of appreciation has slowed. According to one pundit, only Texas experienced any increase in housing values in 1981. Buyers are fewer and farther between these days, in large part because a good mortgage is hard to find.

Despite these changes, it's still sensible to assume that your home will appreciate while you own it. Furthermore, you can safely bet that you will never be taxed on your home's increase in value if you sell it.

Congress could have taxed sales of principal residences as strictly as other kinds of capital gains. Instead, it has juggled the Internal Revenue Code to permit all of us to trade up to more expensive homes without paying a nickel in federal income taxes. This is known as the "rollover" rule. The Code also permits older people (fifty-five or older) to trade down to less expensive housing and establish a larger supply of ready cash.

The rollover rule is fairly simple. You pay no income tax on a profitable sale of your home if you buy another one within two years of the sale and if your replacement home (including improvements you put in) costs at least as much as the net amount you received from the sale of your former home (the sale price minus broker's commission, attorney's fees, and fix-up costs you're obligated to incur as part of the sale). The two-year period is really four years, consisting of the two years on either side of the sale of the old home. It means you can buy the new house and *then* have two years to sell the old one.

The Code gives an even better deal to those of us who are fifty-five or older. If you sell your home after you reach that age, you may exclude from your income the first $125,000 of net profit that you realize from the sale. Consequently, in most cases, older people can sell their homes and buy cheaper places without attracting taxes on the profits that they retain as savings or invest in another medium. The idea behind it is to free older people from large houses after the kids have left the nest.

That summarizes the benefits of home ownership. Unfortunately, there are lots of costs attached to the manor.

► **THE COSTS OF HOME OWNERSHIP**

Unless you are especially well off, you'll have to put close to all of your savings in a down payment and get a mortgage, which leaves you with no cash reserves and means monthly payments of interest and principal to your banker. You'll have to pay real estate taxes and insurance premiums. You may have to pay for your garbage removal, sewer connections, water services, and other kinds of necessities. You'll have to pay for the windows you break, the eaves that get clogged, the mice that want exterminating. You'll spend your free time yakking about how the neighborhood is going to hell. Congratulations! You've bought a piece of the American Dream.

▶ **BENEFITS AND COSTS ANALYZED**

Probably the first question you should ask yourself is whether you ought to own a home. People almost always assume that they should, because real estate appreciates and itemized deductions reduce income taxes. This is *not* always the right assumption to make. If you're in the wrong tax situation, the benefits of home ownership won't be worth the sale price of a cheap suit. For example, you may not have enough itemized deductions to exceed your zero-bracket amount, even with home ownership deductions. In that case, your home ownership deductions have no tax value.

For those of you in higher income brackets, it generally still makes sense to own a home. Anyone who is in a lower bracket should analyze his or her circumstances carefully.

We have devised a formula to help you determine whether you should buy a home. First, we state it concisely. Then we explain it.

You should buy if the taxes you save plus the rent you save plus the appreciation in value of your home are greater than the increased expenses you incur and the after-tax "opportunity cost" (we'll explain the term later) of the purchase.

We've also got a little arithmetic program to go with our formula. You're welcome to use it if you lack the experience to figure out *how* to figure out whether it's worth it for you to buy a home. It is a struggle to apply it, but it is a very useful tool.

First, assume that your home will appreciate (unless you buy over a Florida sinkhole) and the amount of appreciation will not be taxed for all the reasons we mentioned earlier. And now, let's forget about appreciation for the time being, since you can't determine how much of an increase will occur in your case (or in any case, for that matter). We'll come back to it later.

Second, calculate the amount of rent you'll save by buying a home. To do this, multiply your current monthly rent by twelve. That gives you a yearly total.

Third, add the amount of income taxes you will save by home ownership. To get this amount, you have to remember that we're talking about *itemized* deductions here. To achieve any tax savings from itemized deductions, the total you have must exceed the zero-bracket amount (standard deduction) for your filing status. If they don't exceed it, they produce no reduction in your income tax bill.

As a result, you have to:

1. Figure out your itemized deductions without the home (say $2,000).
2. Subtract your zero-bracket amount (say $3,400—we declare you married); the result is a *negative* figure of $1,400.
3. Add the itemized deductions that arise from owning a home (say $4,000). Now we have a positive figure of $2,600.
4. Multiply the extra itemized deductions by your tax bracket (say 30%), meaning your tax bill is reduced by $780.

Now you add this figure to your other savings from home ownership.

Incidentally, you may not know your tax bracket. Here is a fairly easy way to figure it if your income is stable. We aim to be helpful.

Get your last year's tax return and find the line for "taxable income." Then go to the tax guide you got with your blank returns for last year and turn to the page for Schedules X, Y, and Z. Read down the table that applies to your filing status until you reach the range in which your income falls. Next to the range, there will be a statement of tax due plus the percentage rate of taxation on the amount of your taxable income that exceeds the specified amount. That percentage rate is your "marginal federal income tax bracket." Or, if you prefer, it is your "tax bracket." That's the percentage by which you multiply the amount of itemized deductions in excess of your zero bracket to figure out tax savings.

There's one last way to do this and we recommend it only to the compulsives among our readers. If you have a fairly good fix on what your income and deductible expenses will be next year, you can sit down and prepare an experimental tax return for your first year of home ownership and an alternative practice return for next year without income ownership. You can directly compare the two results. Then, if you have some spare time, you can do *our* taxes.

In determining the taxes you save, as an astute observer you will discover one reason why people in higher brackets do better by owning homes than people in lower brackets. Let's assume that you're married and have no children. You and your spouse share a zero-bracket amount of $3,400. Let's also assume that you determine that you'll have a total of $6,000 in itemized deductions if you decide to buy a house. To calculate your tax savings, you subtract $3,400 from $6,000 and multiply the remaining $2,600 by your income tax rate. If you're in the 20% bracket, you'll save $520. If you're in the 30% bracket, you'll save $780 (30% of $2,600 equals $780). In short, the higher your bracket, the more you save.

Once you've calculated and combined rent and tax savings, you know your estimated benefit—still ignoring appreciation—from home ownership. Now you're ready to reduce that gain by the costs of your home. This is the depressing part of the exercise.

Subtract from the gain the following: your real estate taxes; mortgage interest; the cost of property services you pay directly (garbage removal, sewer connections, water, and the like); and home insurance. Those are the obvious parts of your cost. There is another hidden cost that can be sizable.

It comes about because you'll have to make a down payment on your mortgage with a chunk of your savings, perhaps all of your savings. You'll probably pay a broker and a lawyer something as well.

If you didn't use these dollars for a down payment and attendant expenses, you could invest them in some profitable enterprise and get income from the investment. Consequently, you have to add to your costs of home ownership the amount of *after-tax* income you lose by precluding alternate investment of the savings you tie up in purchasing a home. This is the "opportunity cost" we mentioned earlier, and it can be a pretty sizable loss.

The interesting thing here is that people in higher tax brackets lose more by making alternate investments than do people in lower tax brackets. This supports our premise that home ownership is better for higher-bracket people than for lower-bracket people. Sounds backward, does it? Don't worry, we'll tell you why, right now.

Let's assume you'll have to make a $10,000 down payment. If instead you stuck it in a high-yield mutual fund, you might earn 10% on it. If you're in the 20% bracket, your after-tax return would be $800 or 8% on the investment. If you're in the 30% bracket, your after-tax return on the same investment would be $700 or 7% ($10,000 times 10% minus 30% of that 10%). The higher your bracket, the higher the taxation of alternate investments—that's the explanation.

In sum, you've got to reduce the total of rent saved and taxes saved by the amount of income you could earn from the money that you put in the down payment, closing costs, and fix-up costs. The total savings is disappearing quickly, isn't it?

In fact, you've probably got a negative number by now. In the first year, more is going out than is coming in. Are the purported joys of home ownership beginning to pall a bit?

This is when appreciation reenters the picture. Let's assume that in the first year you have $2,000 more going out in after-tax expenses than you have coming back in the form of rent and income taxes saved. You may now conclude that your home must appreciate by at least $2,000 to cover your losses in that first year. If it doesn't, then the purchase isn't worth it, unless you believe that the peace of mind that allegedly goes with home ownership still justifies this economic hemorrhage.

It should be clearer now why home ownership is better for higher-bracket taxpayers than it is for lower-bracket taxpayers. Because of progressive taxation, those of you who are in higher brackets get greater tax savings than earners in lower brackets get from usable itemized deductions. That bias is reinforced by the fact that higher-bracket taxpayers keep less of their income from alternative investments than lower-bracket taxpayers. Those two forces should push people in higher tax brackets toward home ownership and people in lower brackets away from it.

You should also remember that these are estimates of what may happen to you if you purchase a home. You can't predict with any degree of certainty whether the costs and benefits will be what you expect. Things may go better or worse for you than you predict. Since we believe in Murphy's Law, it's probably a good idea to build a margin of error into your calculations. It may hurt, but if you want to be conservative, consider increasing your estimated costs by 5 to 10% and decreasing your estimated benefits by the same amount.

By the way, if you didn't already know what "microeconomic analysis" is, you'll be pleased to know that you just did it. When you prepare alternative budgets based on slightly different assumptions (the tax consequences of renting versus owning your home), you engage in the fine art of microeconomics.

In fact, you can now use the term "opportunity cost" with impunity, too. You determined the opportunity cost of this transaction when you calculated the opportunity for earning investment income that you lost by putting your savings in a down payment and related expenses.

Well done! If you were not already as qualified to be Director of the Budget as the incumbent, you are now.

In the next section, we talk about ownership of purely commercial property. In contrast to deductions for home ownership, everything you gain and lose here occurs above the line. You should be a bit happier about this. We hope you are.

► **OWNERSHIP OF PURELY COMMERCIAL REAL ESTATE**

We'll begin this section with an important observation. When you invest in rental real estate for profit (or tax write-offs), for tax purposes you are either in it as a "business" if you are an active landlord, or you are "holding property for the production of rents" (magic Code words) if you are a passive landlord—that is, if other people sign up the tenants, clean the place, and so on.

In either case, all of the itemized deductions we discussed, such as property taxes and service costs, interest on mortgage or property improvement loans, maintenance, and insurance become above-the-line deductions. You don't have to consider your zero-bracket amount in calculating the worth to you of real estate investments. As a result, it is much easier to figure out the tax consequences of this kind of property.

► **THE DAZZLING WORLD OF REAL ESTATE DEPRECIATION**

In addition to the metamorphosis of itemized deductions into nonitemized deductions, the most significant difference between home ownership of real estate and ownership of rental property or property used in your trade or business is the availability of depreciation. You can't depreciate your home. Don't even think about it. You'll just get swatted.

In contrast, you can depreciate *improved* real estate held for business or rental purposes to the point of zero value. The key word in the last sentence is "improved." Improved real estate generally means buildings and other structures built on the land. Congress likes office buildings and barns. In its eyes, any structure is an improvement, and you can completely write off new or used improvements in fifteen years.

There are two other things to remember about depreciation of improved real estate. First, we all know that most improved real estate does not usually decline in value; it increases in value. It may or may not appreciate at a rate that beats inflation but it does *not* decline in value at the rate of speed the Congress enacted into law recently. It is absurd for that wonderfully deliberative body to permit 100% depreciation of new or used improved real estate on a fifteen-year schedule. Consider, friend, the Parthenon.

Congress compounded the absurdity by allowing any buyer of used improved real estate to start the fifteen-year cycle all over again. When you acquire property that someone else depreciated part of the way or all of the way to zero, you can take the price you paid for the building, divide it by fifteen, and use the result each year to offset your income from the building.

As absurd as depreciation is, it is understandably attractive to economically rational taxpayers. You can prove this by marching into almost any stock brokerage office in the country, where you can feast on a rich diet of tax shelter offerings that hawk investments in real estate through public limited partnership arrangements that restrict your liability to the amount you invest in the

HOW DEPRECIATION WORKS

1975   1980

deal. If you can put up a substantial amount of cash right now (somewhere between $5,000 and $10,000), you may someday get some rental income from the property.

Most of the people who invest in these deals are indifferent to actual rents. The rental stimulus is not the play for the investment; it is the depreciation deductions you can immediately claim to reduce your taxable income in each year you are a partner.

If you flip to the back pages of these enticements, you will find projections that show how much you may expect to receive for each year in current depreciation deductions and other kinds of deductible expenses, especially interest expense incurred by the partnership.

Someday, the partnership will probably sell the real estate in a carefully structured deal and realize a very tidy capital gain, of which you will partake. A lot, perhaps all, of that "gain" will arise

1985   1986

from the fact that the building was written off. That capital gain will be taxed at a rate no greater than 20%. (All join now in chorus: "50% of 40% is 20%.") Furthermore, your capital gain tax will probably have been radically exceeded in prior years by your tax savings from your share of the expenses of the partnership. Those depreciation deductions were 100% deductible, but only 40% of the capital gains is taxed. This is *pure* conversion of ordinary deductions into capital gains. This is tax alchemy. This is lobbying power at work.

Let's look at a down-home illustration. You and a friend decide to form a partnership and buy a small apartment building. The building costs $62,000, of which $60,000 is for the building and $2,000 is for the land. You and your partner each invest cash of $6,000 and borrow the remaining $50,000 from a bank. You are now entitled to "write off" (depreciate) the *entire* purchase price of the building in fifteen years. It doesn't matter whether the building is brand new or ninety-nine years old. If you write it off in equal amounts each year, each of you may claim $2,000 in nonitemized depreciation deductions in each year you own the building ($60,000 divided by fifteen divided by two partners).

When you sell the building someday, your profit is taxed as a capital gain. If you've kept the building in good condition, you can probably sell it for at least what you paid for it. Whatever income you've gotten from the building during the time you owned it (after paying for taxes, the mortgage, insurance, and maintenance) has probably been reduced or erased altogether by "depreciation" deductions. Moreover, the IRS doesn't reduce these deductions just because the building doesn't *really* depreciate. You get to keep the deductions and the resulting tax savings can be put in the bank, even if you merely sell the building for its original purchase price. Let's return to the example.

Fifteen years later, you sell the property for $62,000. Its value has not moved an inch. You realize a $60,000 gain on the building. The tax bill in your bracket (say 50%) times 40% (the capital gains deduction is at work here) times $30,000 (your share), equals $6,000. What taxes did you save in the meantime? The answer is your tax bracket times $30,000, or $15,000. Over the life of your investment, you saved $9,000 in taxes ($15,000— 6,000). Nice going! By the way, this is a favorite pastime of half the population of Beverly Hills.

Up to now, you may have wondered why we gave real estate special treatment. The answer is that it combines just about every tax benefit in the book. It permits you to:

1. Defer income (through current losses, a lot of which—depreciation—are on paper).
2. Convert ordinary deductions into capital gains.
3. Earn tax-free income, by occupying your home, letting it roll over, and then selling it after age fifty-five.
4. Split income (by transferring profitable real estate to lower bracket taxpayers).
5. Earn big tax credits for major rehabilitation of nonresidential property and historic properties generally. The big hook is that the cost of the rehabilitation has to be at least equal to the property's adjusted gross basis. That is a cinch in fifteen years, when it has a $0 adjusted basis. We discuss that in our section on swapping real estate.

There is still *another* attractive feature of real estate. If it is held for business or investment purpose, it can be exchanged for other real estate on a tax-free basis.

► **EQUITY SHARING**

For most people, the biggest obstacle to buying a first home is the down payment. In the past, many young couples have turned to Mom and Dad for that money in the form of a gift. Now, Mom and Dad (or any other angel) can use recent changes in the tax law to finance the down payment in a way that offers them substantial tax benefits.

The magic words are "equity sharing." The gist of the arrangement is that the angel becomes a co-investor and puts up a good share of the down payment, cosigns the mortgage, and charges the occupants an appropriate rent. Because the arrangement turns the angel into an investor, he or she can claim (1) depreciation deductions on his or her share of the property, (2) interest expenses for mortgage payments, and (3) real estate taxes. They are *all* deductible to the angel, but the key piece is the depreciation. In exchange for participating, the angel gets a big piece of the profits (say 50%) when the home is sold. If the angel is in a good mood, he or she can give back the rent as a gift, although doing so is a bit dicey from a tax perspective.

The system works, and it is catching on fast. Diligent real estate brokers know a lot about it, and in some parts of the country public investors are being sought to play the role of angel.

There are also plenty of pitfalls. People and real estate are both unpredictable. As a result, it is *absolutely vital* to have a complete understanding on all points *before* any equity-sharing arrangement is struck. Obvious points include rent charges over the years, how much of the sale price goes to the owner, what happens when the property is refinanced, what happens if either party falls behind in a payment, and buy-out rights, if any.

Now for the brighter side. Here is a conservative example of how the numbers might look in a fairly straightforward equity-sharing deal. Let's assume you find your $100,000 dream home, available for $20,000 down and a 12½% mortgage. You have $10,000 for a down payment and you persuade your rich uncle Fred, the storm-door tycoon, to co-invest as half owner. He puts down $10,000, signs the note, and correctly charges you $350 in rent. Real estate taxes run $2,000 per year. Let's assume for purposes of simplicity that the annual interest charge is $12,500. Fred and you each pays one-half of the taxes and interest.

We have set it out in a table. We hope the results are clear:

Fred has done fairly well. He shows a minor after-tax annual profit, and the hope of a tasty gain when you sell.

How well have you done? Pretty darn well. You paid out $11,450, and saved $1,812 in federal income taxes, for a net cost of $9,638, or $803 per month to live in a nice new home with good hope of a substantial long-term capital gain when you sell it.

▶ **SWAPPING BUSINESS OR INVESTMENT REAL ESTATE**

Let's suppose you own a tiny apartment building in Duluth, Minnesota, where you've lived and worked for your entire life. If you decide to move to Dallas, Texas (or someplace nicer), you can swap the Duluth building for a Dallas building of equal value. You will not recognize any gain on the transaction (and therefore will pay no tax) if you do not get any cash or property other than business or investment real estate.

To do this, you don't have to find someone who wants your property and owns exactly the building in Dallas you want. Your real estate broker can arrange something called a "three-corner exchange."

The first corner is constructed when you put your building on the market in Duluth. You then identify a building in Dallas that you want. Your broker tells a prospective buyer of your property in Duluth to purchase the building you've identified in Dallas. The prospective buyer does and you've turned the second corner. You

ANNUAL RESULTS OF EQUITY SHARING

	Uncle Fred's Costs (Investor)	Your Costs (Occupant)
Mortgage Interest	$ 6,250	$ 6,250
Real Estate Taxes	1,000	1,000
Total	$ 7,250	$ 7,250
Rent to Fred	−4,200	+4,200
Total Annual Expenses	$ 3,050	$11,450

	Uncle Fred's Benefits	Your Benefits
Deduction for Interest Expense	$ 6,250	$ 6,250
Real Estate Taxes	1,000	1,000
Depreciation (½ of cost of home)	3,333	−0−
Total Annual Deduction	$10,583	$ 7,250
Income from Rental	(4,200)	
Net Tax Savings to Uncle Fred (50% tax bracket*)	$ 3,191	
To you (25% tax bracket)		$ 1,812

	Uncle Fred's After-tax Profit on Equity Sharing
Income from Rent	$ 4,200
Taxes Saved	3,191
Annual After-tax Income	$ 7,391
Annual Expenses	$ 7,250
Net Profit	$ 141

* That is: (deductions − rent) × 50% = $10,583 − $4,200 × .5 = $3,191

and your buyer now swap your building in Duluth and his building in Dallas. Neither of you pays any taxes on this exchange. Everything is fine. He has his building in the Frost Belt and you get to make a thorough study of the air conditioner market in Dallas. The gain, of course, is deferred.

The last topic covered in this section on real estate is the hybrid: the kind of building in which you live and which you also use in part for business or investment purposes. We'll touch briefly on the home-office deduction first and then move to a review of other and more beneficial kinds of residential-business property. After that, we discuss vacation homes. This smoothly leads us to the tax advantages of other kinds of recreational property discussed in Chapter Nine. You see, there is a pattern and a plan for your existence. We're here to help you find it. But first, stop reading. Take off. Have some fun.

▶ **HYBRID REAL ESTATE: THE HOME OFFICE**

Welcome back. Most of us are familiar with the home-office deduction permitted by the tax laws. You probably know at least one person who takes it. Large numbers of homeowners and renters use their houses and apartments to conduct their business activities or as the location for part-time work that supplements their primary incomes. By the way, when we say "office," we include places like workshops, small retail areas, and so on.

For many years, Congress has permitted taxpayers to deduct the expenses of running a home office from the income they derived from it. Quite sensibly, Congress chose to treat the expenses of home offices in the same way that it regards all other business expenses. They are nonitemized deductions and reduce gross income from the business on a dollar-for-dollar basis.

Consequently, home offices can be very attractive. If you run a small business on a full- or part-time basis, which doesn't justify the expense of a separate commercial office (or you're just very, very cheap), you can operate out of your home and save a substantial amount of overhead. Subject to some limitations, you can also take the deduction if your employer requires you to keep an office in your home.

We are not about to beat the advantages of the home office to death. In a nutshell, here they are:

1. Some of the domestic expenses that you have anyway become deductible. For example, if your office represents one-quarter of your floor space, you can deduct one-quarter of your garbage removal, utilities, and general upkeep expenses.
2. You can depreciate the office. If you use straight-line depreciation over fifteen years for property acquired after 1980 (or straight-line over some longer period for pre-1981 property),

all of the gain from the sale of the office part of your home is taxable as a capital gain.

3. Other expenses that *are* deductible, such as mortgage interest and local real estate taxes, become deductible "above the line." That may be helpful if you are low on itemized deductions.

On the other hand, the right to claim the deduction is closely confined. If a separate structure is involved, for example, an artist's studio, it must be used regularly and exclusively in connection with a business. If it is part of your home, it must be the principal place of the business carried on there, or be a place where clients, customers or patients regularly come to deal with you. In case you were wondering, the IRS *will* send agents to check out your claim for a home office deduction if the Tax Spirit moves them.

► **THE LIMIT**

There is a limit to the amount of expenses you may deduct. You may not deduct more in home-office expenses than you receive in home-office income. You may have a zero-sum game, but you can't do better than that. That is still not bad. Why? Simple. Because those home-office deductions that you would have anyway reduce your taxable income. In other words, the cash from the business is tax-free to the extent of the new-found deductions.

► **YEAR-ROUND BUSINESS/COMMERCIAL PROPERTY**

We spent a good deal of time on home offices because they're the easiest way to understand the rules for this kind of property. They really aren't very different for other situations in which you mix (but segregate) personal and commercial uses.

Let's suppose that you buy a building with two apartments in it. You move into one apartment and you rent the other one to tenants. We'll also assume that the tenant's apartment is 50% of the square footage of the building.

You may deduct above the line the following:

☐ 100% of all of the expenses that you incur as a result of your tenants' presence in the building;
☐ 50% of all expenses that indivisibly affect the entire building;
☐ 50% of all your other deductions that you incur as a result of

owning the building, and that you would otherwise have to itemize "below the line."

You may deduct the remaining 50% "below the line."

Moreover, you can write off (depreciate) the portion of the building that the tenants live in over a fifteen-year period. For example, you can take the share of the cost of the building (remember: you can't depreciate land) at the time you begin to rent the apartment, divide it by 2 (50% of the building is business) and divide it again by 15, assuming you want to use straight-line depreciation. You may then deduct the result from your income. That alone can substantially reduce your taxable income.

If you sell the building at some later time for more than you paid for it, you'll have to report a capital gain of 50% of the profit on the sale (the price you got for the building minus the price you paid for it, divided by 2). Beware of recapture though. The easy way to avoid it is to stick to straight-line depreciation.

The benefits don't end there. You should also remember that the increase in the value of the *rest* of the property (your share of the building) will not be taxed as a capital gain if, within two years of the sale, you buy a new home that costs at least as much as the amount you got for the Old Homestead.

These arrangements can be made for any kind of rental agreement for any use of any part of your property. You can do it with anything from a spare room to a spare building. Keep good books, observe the legalities, and you won't regret the results.

Before we leave real estate forever, we'll discuss second homes. It may seem a bit peculiar to single them out for specific treatment, but there's a good reason for it. They can be a productive blend of personal residence and apartment building. In other words, they can lend themselves to the kind of reduced taxation we've discussed so far in this chapter.

▶ **SECOND HOMES**

If you don't own a second home, we suggest that you read Thorstein Veblen instead of this section, so that you can understand the complex social forces that drive our citizens to worship the god of conspicuous consumption. Or, you can just recognize that play is better than work, at least for people who aren't crazy, leave it at that, and read on.

If you do own a second home or are thinking about one, you can use it as part of your tax strategy, but you have to be willing to lease all or part of it to someone else for a part of the year. You can skip this section altogether if you aren't excited by the prospect of people paying you for the privilege of burning holes in your furnishings or bringing mud, snow, or sand inside to ruin your floors.

Now that we've warned off the frivolous readers, the few of us who remain can consider this subject in detail. With certain differences that we'll mention as we go along, vacation homes are treated like any other hybrid real estate that you use for personal and commercial purposes. You can think of vacation homes as apartment buildings with short-term tenants who compete with you for space. Consequently, you can deduct from your gross rental income a portion of the costs you incur to own and maintain the building.

At this point, we have to introduce you to two critical phrases, so hold your nose. The phrases are "vacation-home rules" and "hobby-loss rules."

The vacation-home rules provide that you may not report losses from rentals of habitable property if you personally use the property for more than the *greater of* 14 days or 10% of the rental period. The hobby-loss rules disallow losses from activities that you do not genuinely undertake to make a profit.

Now we'll show you how those rules are applied. Follow along.

The tax aspects of a second home fall into three categories, depending on how much of the year you rent it. There are three rules:

1. If you rent it for fourteen days or less, you don't have to report the income, but you also get no deductions other than the ones everyone gets: namely, below-the-line deductions for interest, property taxes, and casualty losses. The result is tax-free income. Nice, but not spectacular.
2. If you rent it a lot, but don't use it much yourself, you can report losses, provided you are really in it for a profit (the hobby-loss rules at work). The profit may come from renting or selling the property. To do this, you may not use it for more the greater of 14 days or 10% of the rental period (the vacation-home rules at work).
3. If you rent it for more than 14 days, but use it "too much" from the Congress's point of view (over both the 14-day and 10% limits), the vacation-home rules prohibit you from re-

porting losses. Period. On the other hand, all of your rents will probably escape taxation.

These three rules constitute the essence of the "hobby-loss" and "vacation home" rules. In fact, like everything else in the Code, they are more complicated than that, but our explanation will tell you what to watch for when you have a second home. By the way, the rules apply to time-sharing and ownership-pooling arrangements.

The vacation home rules were amended in 1981 to make renting to family members or others far less touchy. Under the 1981 changes, use of the property as a principal residence by a member of your family or a co-owner who is a partner does not count in "personal use" by yourself, as long as you and the user are jointly liable on any debt on the property.

Bored? Don't stop. Here's the tax strategy, by example.

An example: Pop is getting older. Pop transfers the home to Sis and himself as joint tenants. Sis charges Pop rent, but pays and deducts the whole mortgage interest and claims depreciation on her half.

The effect is to give older members of the family needed cash, but usually no tax, because people fifty-five years or older can exclude the first $125,000 of gain. The younger generation can manufacture deductions for depreciation and interest expenses, and can, thanks to the new relaxation of the vacation home rules, report a loss for income tax purposes.

Now let's put the tax advantages of a second home into capsule form, and move on:

1. You hold an investment that, when sold, generates a capital gain. To the extent you can claim straight-line depreciation deductions in earlier years, you can convert those fully deductible paper expenses into a favorably taxed long-term capital gain.

2. The use of the place is tax-free, although you must reduce your deductions by the percentage of the total use which is personal. That goes for all expenses other than real estate taxes, interest, and casualty losses.

3. You can defer your gains for as long as you want.

4. The cash you earned from the rentals will almost invariably be offset by your maintenance and depreciation expenses.

5. You can get hefty tax credits for installing energy saving devices in rental homes, if the property is held for transient

rentals (less than thirty days). If you happen to be able to latch on to a historic property in grave need of repairs, you can get a tax credit equal to 25% of the cost of rehabilitating the place. That is simply phenomenal. Credits are lovable because after *at most* a five-year wait they are yours forever.

Enough. Our next stop is the tax benefits of portable property. With apologies to Mr. Hemingway, we call it "The Movable Feast."

CHAPTER *Nine*

9 | THE

MOVABLE

FEAST:

AIRPLANES,

BOATS,

CAMPERS,

MOTOR HOMES,

AND CARS

―――――

"A table of the Movable Feasts"
BOOK OF COMMON PRAYER

―――――

For PEOPLE who purchase and lease to others property like sailboats and power boats, airplanes, mobile homes, and cars, the tax laws offer lush but poorly understood benefits. They are similar to those we've discussed for commercial uses of real estate, except that there is no conversion of ordinary deductions into capital gains. On the *plus* side, there is an investment tax credit.

► **ITC BENEFITS AND RECAPTURE OF THE ITC**

The easiest benefit to obtain and understand is an old acquaintance: the investment tax credit (ITC), which is a fixed percentage of the purchase price you pay for the property. (You were formally introduced in principle #8 of Chapter Two.) The credit applies to "tangible personal property held for the production of rents," as well as to business property.

"Tangible personal property" describes things that you touch, feel, and hold and that are not species of "real property." Land, and the improvements you make on land, are "real property." Except for certain major rehabilitations, you generally can't claim the investment tax credit for real property.

"Rent-producing purposes" is easy to define. This simply means that the property will be leased out to the rest of the world.

As we mentioned before, the investment tax credit is a very effective way to reduce your tax bill. After you compute your taxable income and determine the tax on that income, you subtract the credit on a dollar-for-dollar basis from the amount of tax you would otherwise have to pay.

You'll also remember that you may take the full credit in the year of purchase but that different kinds of property earn different amounts of credit over different periods of time. To earn and retain the full credit, you must keep the property for the number of years that applies to the kind of property. If you don't, the IRS will recapture the portion of the credit that you did not earn by premature disposal of the property.

For example, you purchase a car for $8,000. Because cars get a 6% investment tax credit, you may deduct $480 (6% of $8,000) from your tax bill for the year in which you purchase the car. If you keep the car for three years, you retain the full credit. If you sell it after two years, you must refund $160 (one-third of the credit). To put it another way, you "earn" the credit at a rate of 2% per year. Under the last round of tax law changes, you must reduce your basis (i.e., the cost for depreciation purposes) by half the credit.

The investment tax credit was designed to stimulate industrial production and the purchase of new business equipment. In fact, it was written so oafishly that it encompasses used tangible personal property and is by no stretch of the imagination restricted to industrial equipment. Moreover, you can take the full credit even if you finance the purchase. The government doesn't care whether you paid cash out of your pocket or obtained 99.9% financing. You take the full credit in either case, provided you are personally liable for at least 20% of the debt and borrowed it from an unrelated person.

▶ **THE ITC RECAPTURE PROBLEM**

If you sell a boat or other personal property before the full life you claimed for setting the ITC, you have to recapture the part of the credit you "overclaimed." For example, if you claimed a $1,000 ITC for a boat, and sold it after four years, you would have overclaimed the actual credit by 20%, because boats are on the five-year ITC schedule. That means you owe the Treasury 20% of the credit, or $200. It's true you just got a tax-free loan, but you must pay the Federal piper all the same.

▶ **DEPRECIATION**

Because you're using the property for business or production of rents, the second major benefit you get is the right to depreciate its cost. You may depreciate it to zero value on the same schedule that applies to the investment tax credit, or you may elect to write it off over a longer period of time.

This produces absolutely extraordinary results. If you purchase a car for your business and drive it for a total of three miles over three years, you can still depreciate the entire cost of the car.

You can also claim a so-called "section 179 expense." Specifically, if you buy property used in your business, you can write off $5,000 worth of such property at once. The rest has to be written off over the regular depreciation period. The $5,000 rises slowly to $10,000 in 1986 and thereafter. Generally, as long as you are actively involved in renting out your boat (or car, van, trailer, airplane, etc.), you get the right to claim section 179 expenses.

▶ **THE DEPRECIATION RECAPTURE PROBLEM**

There is a price for all this. If you sell the property for less than its original cost, but more than its adjusted basis, that portion of the gain is taxed as ordinary income. If you sell it for more than you paid, the excess over what you originally paid is generally taxed as a capital gain.

An example. Let's say you bought a boat for $10,000, and you lease it to the public. You may immediately take an investment tax credit of $1,000, because boats are deemed to have a five-year life and are therefore on the 10% investment credit schedule. Under the 1982 law, you have to reduce the cost of the boat by half the credit (i.e., by $500), unless you voluntarily take an 8% credit. This means you can write off only $9,500 of the cost, not the full $10,000. You hold the boat for five years and depreciate it to zero value during that time by one-fifth a year (or some other formulae). At the end of the five years, you sell the boat for $15,000. The $5,000 excess over your purchase price is taxed at capital gain rates. That means you exclude $3,000 from income (60% of the $5,000). But here is the problem. The first $10,000 which you received is taxed as ordinary income. That hurts. If you sold it for only $10,000, then the full $10,000 gain is treated as ordinary income.

In other words, the portion that is taxed as ordinary income equals the amount by which you depreciated the property below the price you paid for it. Any amount you receive in excess of the purchase price is generally taxed as a capital gain.

Usually, you can avoid any problem of ordinary income by exchanging the property. The usual exchange is simply a trade-in for a newer and shinier piece of the same kind of property.

► **INTEREST EXPENSE DEDUCTIONS AND IMPUTED INCOME**

The third benefit you may pull out of this sack comes about if you finance the purchase. Once again, the Code permits you to deduct from income the interest expense of the loan you used to acquire the property. If it is used in business, or held for the production of rents, then you deduct the interest "above the line."

These three deductions are always available. The hobby-loss rules and vacation-home rules that limit deductions for real property do not apply here.

► **IMPUTED INCOME**

The final advantage is that the government does not tax the pleasure you get from the personal use of the property when you're not leasing it to someone else. Your enjoyment is treated as "imputed income," the kind the government has decided not to tax. This imputed income does not affect your basic right to claim interest expense deductions and deductions for property taxes. You must, however, reduce the allowable investment tax credit, deductible depreciation, and deductible maintenance expenses to the extent of the portion of the time you use the boat for personal pleasure.

Here's how the reduction works. Let's suppose that you purchase a boat for $20,000. You expect to use it for personal purposes on fifty days each year and rent it out for 200 days. One-fifth (or 20%) of your use will be personal. In the first year, you can claim an investment tax credit of $1,600 (80% of 10% of $20,000). Assuming your estimate of rental income is borne out in later years (and you don't have tax problems that we get into later), you may therefore deduct 80% of your depreciation and maintenance expenses. You may still deduct from gross rental income 100% of your interest expenses and 100% of your local property taxes imposed on the boat. Granted, the reduction is bad. You lost some of the credit, and some deductions, but if you did some comparison shopping you would generally find that the lost tax benefits were much smaller than the cost of renting a comparable boat.

For the rest of this chapter, we're going to stick with boats because they blend many of these rules and are very popular instruments for sheltering taxable income, and because the same rules apply to campers, airplanes and other equipment. Besides, most of the planet (and most of us) is water.

There are two basic ways to go about mixing personal and

commercial uses of boats. The low budget way is to buy a boat yourself and lease it by yourself. The high budget method involves buying it and renting it through a commercial boat brokerage firm. We'll start with the personal method and then move to the more complex commercial arrangements.

► **DOING IT ON YOUR OWN**

Let's suppose you, your spouse, and your children live in Maine during the summer. You buy a boat that you can sleep aboard and offer to lease it to the public. Your children can help out in the business.

Because you're directly in the business of leasing, you may claim an investment tax credit, and deduct depreciation, maintenance expenses, salaries, insurance, and all other expenses for the boat that are attributable to the commercial usage.

If you are really in it for a profit, you can report a loss, unless you use the habitable boat for more than *both* 14 days *and* 10% of the rental period. If you exceed both limits, you can't report a loss for tax purposes. This is that old harpie, the vacation-home rule.

You and your family may use the boat too; all you need to do is keep track of the percentage of annual use that is personal and chop down your deductible expenses (other than taxes and interest) by a like percentage. The difficult part is predicting the percentage of personal use by which you must reduce the investment tax credit. For each other expense, you may calculate your "personal deductible" at the end of each summer of rentals.

As a result of all of this, you get a very pleasant trade-off. You and your family have the enjoyment of the boat as often as you want; your personal use is subsidized in part by your customers and the operation of the tax laws.

After five years, your boat no longer generates useful depreciation and there will be no recapture of the investment tax credit. The book value is zero. Most of the rental income is now exposed to taxation. At this point, you have several alternatives. You can sell the boat, trade it for a new one, or keep the boat and continue as before.

The worst alternative is selling the boat. You'll remember that if you sell it for more than the adjusted basis, the full difference between the price at which you sell it and the price you paid for it will be taxed as ordinary income.

For example, you buy a boat for $15,000. Ignoring ITC issues, you depreciate it to zero value. If you sell it for $16,000, $15,000 will be treated as ordinary income, and $1,000 will be taxed according to capital gains rules. You've got the makings of a crushing tax bill, unless you're trying to average your income by pumping up the fifth year of a five-year averageable period. (See Chapter Three on income averaging.)

You can keep the boat, but stop renting it. Surprise! There is also recapture, equal to its value minus its "adjusted basis" ($0) because removing depreciable property from a business or rental-producing status to personal status is generally considered the same as a sale. This rule does *not* apply to property bought before 1981, or if you bought it from a family member, partner, or certain others, after 1981. It will now produce more taxable income unless you find new expenses to offset the income; if you decide to keep it, you could give it to a poor relation (i.e., child) to rent it. That's about it from the tax planning point of view, unless you embark on a major series of repairs or improvements. Gifts don't trigger recapture of depreciation as ordinary income. The moral is that the Tax Man Giveth and the Tax Man Taketh Away. The incentives to buy things to lease out generally force you to stick with the Thing, to dump it in a low bracket year (leveling tax rates), or to give it away (income shifting).

If you do want to get rid of the boat, the best way to do that is to trade it in or swap it for another one. When you find one you like, trade the old one in, pay some additional cash, and put your new boat into business.

The bad news is that you may only depreciate the extra cash cost you paid for your acquisition. To put it another way, suppose your new boat is priced at $15,000. You received a credit of $5,000 toward the purchase as your trade-in allowance for your old boat. The $10,000 cash difference is the purchase price for purposes of depreciation. You may not use the $15,000 price as the basis for depreciation. The result is obvious; you have smaller amounts of depreciation to deduct from rental income in each year and a smaller investment tax credit ($1,000 at most). Otherwise, the rules are unchanged.

▶ **YACHT-LEASING DEALERS**

If you don't want to run the business yourself you can use a commercial brokerage scheme. The back pages of boating magazines are filled with advertisements for brokerage arrangements.

They all share the same basic characteristics. Yacht dealers offer to sell boats to buyers at slightly inflated prices, but they also promise to lease the boat back from the buyer for a number of years, usually three. During those three years, the yacht dealer will lease the boat to the public at fair market rates (or whatever they can get). The boat owner has the right to use the boat during the off season.

The dealer pays a generous rent to the owner for the right to lease the boat to the public. The dealer usually claims that the owner may report an investment tax credit to offset taxes in the year of purchase and depreciation expenses to reduce the taxable income the owner gets from leasing the boat to the dealer.

At the end of the leaseback period, the owner and his boat are kicked out of the leasing fleet. Presumably, the owner picks up where the dealer left off, uses the boat, and makes a tidy income from rentals.

The attractions are (1) all sorts of hyperbole to the effect that the owner can claim an investment tax credit equal to 10% of the purchase price of the boat; (2) the dealers frequently finance these transactions, giving owners significant interest expense deductions; (3) the owners may also use the new accelerated depreciation schedules to offset rental income and write the value of the boat down to zero in five years (or longer, if the owner's tax plan makes a longer write-off schedule worthwhile); and, (4) the owner gets free use of the boat in the off season.

Along this same coast lies a series of reefs guaranteed to send the inattentive owner to Davey Jones' locker. Let's look at them.

First of all, you may not claim *any* investment tax credit if the boat is primarily used outside the Fifty States, unless the boat is either owned by a corporation organized in, or a citizen of, a possession (e.g., the U.S. Virgin Islands), or is registered for use in the "domestic or international United States." The latter term appears to mean that the boat must be inspected and certified according to a tough set of rules enforced by the Coast Guard. Fine, you say, what about keeping it in Florida?

The answer is that even if the boat is properly registered, the tax laws deny the investment tax credit to investors (i.e., human beings) unless the *owner's* business expenses equal at least 15% of the first year's rental income. It is impossible for owners in a dealer's fleet to claim these expenses because of the plain fact that the owner is not in the business of leasing and does not pay the expenses of the fleet; the *dealer* does. The owner can't claim expenses unless there is some sort of arrangement where the owner receives net income *after* expenses, or the dealer gives the owner a check for rental income and a bill for expenses. Even then, it really just seems a sham.

The only other way to deal with this is to have the dealer claim the investment tax credit and give you a reduced purchase price in exchange. We won't spend any more time on this here, but have your tax advisor take a careful look at Section 46(e) of the Code if you're thinking of joining a fleet.

With unhappiness, we report that the problems don't end if and when you've gotten over these first hurdles. The so-called hobby-loss rules will prevent you from reporting a loss unless you intend to make a profit from this arrangement. You must intend to make money in this arrangement.

If the boat is habitable, then the tax laws will further constrain your efforts to claim a loss if you make "excessive personal use" of the boat. You'll remember that we used that term in our discussion of vacation homes. The key rule is that you cannot claim losses based on maintenance or depreciation expenses if you personally use the boat for both more than fourteen days each year and for more than 10% of its actual public rental period. This means that you've got to restrict your use of the boat so that you circumnavigate the vacation home rules and that you've got to intend to make a profit to avoid application of the hobby-loss rules. People who leap into the business of buying boats rarely consider these limitations, and they wind up paying for their shortsightedness.

As we said, these agreements usually run for three years. We also mentioned that the investment tax credit on boats is earned on a five-year schedule. There's a two-year gap here where very bad things may happen to you.

The tax laws say that if your boat is kicked out of the fleet and returned to personal use, you will owe the government the portion of your tax credit that you have not yet earned before the credit has been fully earned. That's not pleasant and it may not be the only or worst penalty, because the new law makes it clear that you also suffer depreciation recapture. That is, the law pretends that you sold the boat at its fair market value. We talked about that little beauty a few pages back.

The solution to both of these problems is to turn the boat over to another fleet if you can find one, or to continue to lease it yourself. Those are very simple ways to avoid recapture, but you need to be aware of the problem and plan to avoid it.

You have more control in an arrangement where you own and

lease the boat. The disadvantage is that you bear the costs of management and operation. You can forget about the costs when you buy a boat and lease it back to the seller, but you're at the mercy of your own skills and energy after you are evicted.

You should consider all these matters when you plan to buy and lease a boat or other similar property. You don't want to go down with the ship if you can avoid it.

► **OTHER PROPERTY**

What we just said about leasing your own boat is equally true of campers and vans. The trouble is, we don't know of anyone who sells them to buyers and then leases them back. The key point about campers is that you can inhabit them. That means the "vacation home" rule and the 14-day–10%-limit on personal use applies.

Cars and airplanes are a bit easier. You can't realistically inhabit them. Otherwise, they offer the same basic benefits and burdens. You can often find airplane sellers who will act as agents to lease them for you.

► **SUMMARY**

Let's add up the pluses and minuses of these offerings. On the plus side:

1. You can claim an investment tax credit. That is a huge government subsidy. You can get the whole subsidy if you are patient.
2. You can always deduct interest, personal property taxes, and casualty losses. That's good. These deductions are *above* the line.
3. You can show losses based on depreciation and maintenance expenses if you really intend to make a profit and, if the Thing is habitable, you don't use it in violation of the 14-day–10%-limit.
4. Your own use of the Thing is not taxed to you. Instead, it is "imputed income."

In other words, you get a fat government subsidy and cheap personal use. Also, you can always rent your Thing for two weeks and settle for the tax-free income, but that means no deductions for depreciation and maintenance, and no ITC.

On the minus side:

1. If you don't seem serious, your losses will be denied.
2. If you convert the Thing to personal use, you get fried. The excess of the Thing's value at that point over its adjusted basis is ordinary income. That makes it a tax deferral device *plus* a subsidy in the form of the ITC, if you were patient. You can escape by giving the Thing to a lower bracket family member, before he or she converts it to personal use, but this form of income shifting is expensive.
3. Renting out Things can be a huge hassle. If you get into it, you are pretty well committed. Before you leap, be honest with yourself about your willingness to stick with it.

CHAPTER  Ten

	10	TAX-FREE
		INCOME:
		BONDS,
		DIVIDENDS,
		AND
		LIFE
		INSURANCE

_____

And it came to pass in those days, that there went out
a decree from Caesar Augustus, that all the world should be taxed.
LUKE 2:1

_____

BY THIS POINT in the primer, it should be clear that the tax laws are designed to encourage and discourage certain sorts of economic activities. Some kinds of activities produce ordinary income; others produce capital gains. Some business arrangements are taxed stringently while others can operate at a very low tax rate.

The best way to stimulate investment in an activity is to prohibit any federal taxation of the income from the investment. Boy, is that the best way!

In this chapter we discuss three popular ways to earn tax-free income: state and local bonds; purchases of stock in companies that pay out dividends-that-are-not-dividends; and life insurance.

There are two related questions you have to answer before you throw money into a tax-free investment: Is it worth it? Can you make more money by investing in taxable activities?

There's a short answer to both questions. The value to you of tax-free investment increases as you move into higher tax brackets.

Let's compare two cases. In both, we'll assume that you have $1,000 to invest and you are trying to choose between a tax-free investment that pays you a 10% return and a taxable investment that pays the same return.

If you're in the 20% bracket, for example, the tax-free investment produces $100 of tax-free income and the taxable investment produces $80 of after-tax income. If you're in a higher bracket, let's say 25%, you will get the same return from the tax-free investment but you will keep only $75 after taxes on the investment.

The tax-free returns always stays the same; your bracket doesn't matter. Your bracket can make a _big_ difference when you're thinking of taxed investments. If you're in the 20% bracket, you have to make $12.50 to keep $10. If you're in the 50% bracket, you have to make $20 to keep $10.

In other words, you have to consider your tax bracket when choosing between tax-free and taxed investments. To make this decision easier, we have for you another little microeconomic program.

This one has two parts and both of them are very easy. In the first part, you calculate the return from a tax-free investment. If you're thinking of buying a $1,000 bond that annually pays 10%, divide $1,000 by 10. Nothing could be easier. Well, almost nothing. The result had better be $100.

The next step allows you to determine the taxed investment you have to make to get the same $100 after taxes. Divide the $100 by 100% minus your marginal tax rate.

For example, if you're in the 33% bracket, divide $100 by 67%. The result will be $150. If you're in the 33% bracket, you have to make $150 *before* taxes to have $100 *after* taxes. You can verify this by multiplying $150 by 33%. You will see that the government will take approximately $50 of that $150 and leave you $100, the same amount you would have earned from your tax-free bond that paid 10%.

Now that we've established this, let's get specific. We'll start with bonds, the favorite of blue-bloods everywhere. Ah, bonds!

▶   **TAX-FREE BONDS**

The most popular form of tax-free investment is the government bond. Specifically, we're referring to bonds issued by state governments and their subdivisions: regional, county, and municipal governments and agencies.

These units of government offer bonds to the public to raise funds for general expenses and specific projects. The governments make two promises about the bonds: they will pay interest on them for a period of years and, at the end of the period (called the "date of maturity"), they will pay back to the holder the full amount of the bond. That's called "redeeming" the bond. In short, governmental bonds are public IOUs that earn interest. Because they produce income that is free from federal income taxes, they offer lower rates of interest than taxable bonds, which must offer market rates of return to be attractive.

Governments prefer to raise funds with bonds instead of taxes. Voters have to pay taxes; they don't have to buy bonds. Taxes make voters mad. Bonds make voters happy, or at least happier than taxes make them.

In most cases, the interest income on these bonds is exempt from federal taxation. You don't even have to report it. You may cash your interest checks and go directly to the track. The IRS won't even notice, unless you bet on the right nags.

Of course the government doesn't tax the money that is returned to you when the bond matures. You or the person who gave you the money to buy the bond have already paid taxes in order to get it.

This tax exemption is based on the constitutional principle that the federal government and state governments are separate sovereign bodies. Neither can tax income from investments in the other's activities. If they could, it would be a lot harder to raise money for government operations. This could be labeled the "you scratch my boondoggles and I'll scratch yours" method of intergovernmental taxation.

Bonds can be very good investments but, for several reasons, they are difficult for amateur investors to manage. First, it is hard to study the bond markets. There are literally thousands of bond issues and it is impossible to keep track of the economic stability of the governments that issue them. You want to buy bonds issued by governments that are and will stay solvent. We don't think we have to do more here than to say the words "New York City" for you to understand our point.

The second characteristic of bonds makes things really complex. The bond markets would be relatively simple to follow if governments issued the bonds and they were bought by people who held them for the full period of maturity and then redeemed them. A fairly large number of people do that, but a lot don't.

For one reason or another, people decide to sell their bonds before they mature. They may need the cash or want to free it for a better investment. At the same time, there are other people who want to buy the used bonds, perhaps because they are issued by solvent governments and offer good returns.

The interest rates on the bonds are generally fixed. If prevailing rates of interest rise because money is scarcer or inflation is reducing its value, old bonds issued with rates lower than the prevailing rates are not going to be attractive.

If you want to sell a bond with a relatively low interest rate, you're going to have to make it attractive. You do that by selling the bond at a price below its actual face value. That's called "discounting" the bond. If you have a bond that has an interest rate that is higher than the prevailing rates, you'll have a lot of bidders. You'll be able to charge a premium for it.

Consequently, bond markets for new and used issues are very sensitive to interest rates. As interest rates rise, the underlying value of bonds declines. If the rates fall, bonds increase in value. Bonds change in value on a day-to-day basis.

To minimize these fluctuations, governments recently have begun to sell interesting bonds called "floaters." The rates of interest paid to purchasers of these bonds vary with the prevailing rates of interest ("float"). As interest rates move, these bonds remain reasonably steady in value. A more recent variation is the "put bond," which lets the purchaser force the seller to buy it back at the original purchase price some years after the purchase, but before the date of maturity.

Another problem arises because buying and selling used immature bonds can yield taxable income. It's not ordinary income. These transactions can produce long- and short-term capital gains and losses from premiums and discounts, which must then be reported and taxed accordingly. The gains from long-term holdings are taxed relatively favorably, but they are still taxed.

For these reasons, the bond markets can be bewildering investments. You're generally better off putting your bond strategies in the hands of professional managers who do nothing but follow bond markets and try to make sense of them. These managers operate municipal bond mutual funds. What you buy are shares in the fund. These funds try to minimize risk by investing in a huge array of bonds.

There are many municipal bond mutual funds; they'll almost always do a better job of managing a bond portfolio than you will. One note: there's no reason to use a fund that charges you a commission (called a "load") for its transactions on your behalf. There are plenty of "no-load" funds that will provide excellent guidance. Stick with them. Also, buy "open-end" funds. We'll get to them in a second.

There is a second form for bond investment that has acquired popularity in recent years. It's called the "unit investment trust." These are municipal bond mutual funds with fixed portfolios of bonds. Their operators promise very high rates of interest but the composition of the portfolio cannot be changed. You can do very well if the bonds in the portfolio are strong and stay strong. You can take a beating if the bonds in the portfolio collapse in value, which will happen if interest rates go up. Some of these trusts invest in "floaters." That means much more safety.

It is very difficult to sell shares in these trusts. They tend to do well in their early years, but they can be albatrosses over the long haul. Usually, there is not much of a market for these shares. It is much easier to buy and sell shares in regular mutual funds than in unit investment trusts. There are thriving markets for them.

In addition, many funds redeem their shares on demand. These are called "open-end" funds. Those that don't redeem on demand are called "closed-end" funds. The closed-end funds generally offer higher rates of return, but the "open-end" funds are more flexible vehicles for investment, because you have at least one certain buyer of your shares if you want to bail out.

► **TAX-FREE-DIVIDENDS-THAT-ARE-NOT-DIVIDENDS**

The tax laws state that dividends paid from stock in corporations are taxable income. Of course, they are not 100% taxable; an individual taxpayer may exclude $100 of dividends from income and taxpayers who file joint returns may exclude from income $200 of dividends. As we mentioned earlier, corporations may typically exclude 85% (sometimes more) of every dividend dollar they receive from taxable income. Whatever is left after the exclusions is taxed at the rate that applies to the taxpayer's total ordinary income.

In this rule, there is a loophole large enough to accommodate Moby Dick. The Code defines taxable dividends as distributions by corporations that have "earnings and profits." In plain American, "having earnings and profits" means "making money." Never forget that. If the entity does not make money, its distributions are not treated as taxable dividends. The distributions are treated instead as returns of a portion of the purchase price you paid for the stock. Because you have been taxed on those dollars before, the government cannot do it again.

On the face of it, this looks like a rotten deal. You'd think that there's no point in investing in a company that is selling unprofitable products or has managers who are too dumb to make a profit.

Appearances are deceiving. It is often difficult to compute earnings and profits, especially in large and diversified companies. These computations do not always reflect reality. For perfectly legal reasons, many companies look terrible on paper but have perfectly satisfactory cash flows.

For example, let's suppose you purchase 1,000 shares of stock in Fred's Storm Door Company for $1,000. The company is selling truckloads of doors but it has recently acquired lots of new and expensive equipment. Consequently, its balance sheet shows enough tax credits, depreciation, and other expenses to offset completely all of its gross receipts. The company is able to pay all of its bills, but the depreciation wipes out the rest of its gross income *on paper*. That gross income is still there in fact. It's in the bank and growing steadily.

The company doesn't show a profit, but its managers don't want that cash earning taxable income for the corporation. They decide to distribute it to shareholders. They declare a *"distribution"* (*not* a dividend) of 10 cents per share. There's no point in the company or anyone else paying taxes on this money, right? Right!

Because you hold 1,000 shares, you will receive $100. This distribution is not taxable as dividend income. It is called a "return of capital."

Nothing else happens and nothing will happen unless and until you decide to sell your shares. If you do sell them, the Code requires you to use $900 as the price you paid for the stock when you compute your capital gain or loss ($1.00 per share minus ten cents per share times 1,000 shares). If you sell the stock at a loss, you will have a smaller capital loss than if the price you used was $1.00. If you sell the stock for more than ninety cents per share, you will have profited more than if the basis for computing the gain were $1.00. Without that distribution that reduced your effective purchase price, you would have been able to report a capital loss on sales for less than $1.00 but more than 90 cents.

This seems to be an obscure species of poetic justice. Your dividend-that-was-not-a-dividend has produced a capital-gain-or-loss-that-is-not-a-capital-gain-or-loss. This has the makings of a zen koan.

You won't have to worry about taxable income if you never sell the stock. This kind of distribution is tax-free. You'll get a stream of dollars that you can reinvest in additional shares of Fred's Company or in other enterprises.

Because sales of stock are treated as capital transactions producing gains or losses, the tax burden is going to be relatively light anyway. Under the new tax law, you will never pay more than a 20% tax on the gain in the value of stock held for more than one year. And, if you don't remember why, you seem to have missed the first nine chapters.

These kinds of distributions may or may not work to your advantage. In the short run, you have a nontaxable return on your investment. However, you can't assess the long-range tax consequences until you think about selling the stock. Depending on your circumstances, you may do very well with this kind of investment. The victory will be yours if you get a good steady flow of nontaxable distributions and you sell the stock for about what you paid for it. Public utility stocks are the most popular vehicle for this strategy.

► **LIFE INSURANCE**

We've delayed the inevitable as long as we could. We'll talk about life insurance now.

With all due respect to a very successful industry, life insurance is an unseemly business. As someone once said about buying life insurance, "You win if you lose and you lose if you win."

Life insurance does have two advantages. It produces two kinds of tax-free income and allows you to defer income as well.

First, we'll define the kinds of life insurance you can use to defer income. There are two basic kinds: "term" insurance and "whole life" insurance.

Term insurance is the classic form. During your lifetime, you regularly pay to the insurance company increasing premiums for a policy that pays a fixed amount. Upon your death, the insurance company pays the face value of the policy, tax-free, to your named beneficiary or beneficiaries.

Whole life insurance describes insurance policies that have death benefits (like term insurance) plus a kind of investment account called the "cash value" of the policy. The amount of the cash value is a function of the number of premiums you've paid, the size of the premiums, the length of time over which you've paid them, and the face value of the policy. If you have a whole-life policy, you can borrow against the whole-life policy.

You may not want to touch these things with a ten-foot pole. Nevertheless, they have several significant tax benefits.

First, the death proceeds are not treated as taxable income for the beneficiary. The proceeds are tax-free.

Second, you can purchase a term life insurance policy with money that you borrow from a whole-life policy. You can get two policies for the price of one. Oh, hurray! Moreover, you may also deduct the interest expense that is charged on loans from the whole-life policy (or any other kind of loan) that you use to finance the policy, but only if you pay four of the first seven premiums on the term policy out of your own pocket.

The third advantage of life insurance is that dividends paid to the insured on the life insurance policy are not taxable. Yes, life insurance policies pay dividends; insurance companies take your premiums and invest them in all kind of profit-making activities, so they'll have enough money to pay your beneficiary when the bell tolls for thee. The insurance companies can pay their policy-holders tax-free dividends on these investments, while the policy-holder is alive.

Be careful in selecting a company or policy; not all insurance companies or policies can do this. The policy must be issued by a mutual insurance company or be a "participating" policy. Furthermore, the dividend histories of the companies vary greatly. Even very big insurance companies can make very dumb investments, and their dividend histories prove it.

That finishes off this exegesis on tax-free income. Now, we go back to taxable income. Our first stop is securities transactions: buying and selling stocks and bonds to defer, convert, and leverage income.

11 SECURITIES

TRANSACTIONS

Our watchword is security.
W. PITT, THE ELDER

REMEMBER THIS: We'll be talk-
ing about the stock market in this chapter. The stock market is Las
Vegas for people who don't care for loud shirts and floor shows,
but the odds still favor the house.

The market manufactures gains and losses more or less ran-
domly. It generates brokers' commissions constantly. Keep that in
mind when you include the market in your plans.

We already discussed some of the tax benefits related to investments in stocks and bonds. You can earn capital gains that are
taxed at lower rates than ordinary income, you can invest in tax-
free bonds, and you can receive dividends that aren't dividends.

You can also leverage investments in securities. You may borrow money to finance securities purchases, and you can deduct the
interest expense of the loan from taxable income. However, you
can't deduct the interest if the bonds you buy are tax-free government obligations.

There are also tax benefits that come directly from the way in
which you time these transactions. There are several timing strategies that can favorably affect your taxable income.

► **LONG-TERM GAINS**

The simplest and most obvious securities strategy constitutes the
choice of long-term capital gains over short-term gains. Long-term
gains—purchases and profitable sales of stock that are separated
by a year and a day or more—are taxed at much more favorable
rates than ordinary income or short-term gains. That is, only 40%
of the gain is taxed. That is why Wall Street is always pushing for
making the long-term holding period as short as possible.

► **PURCHASING DISCOUNTED BONDS**

A second simple and popular strategy is to purchase discounted
bonds with borrowed money. There are a lot of older long-term

bonds that pay interest at very low rates. For example, there are bonds issued around 1950 that mature in the year 2000 and pay 2% interest during the term. Interest rates are now much higher than 2% and, as a result, these 2% bonds are very unattractive. It is a near certainty that you can buy these bonds at an extremely discounted rate. Nobody wants them. They're orphans.

The trick is to borrow to buy these bonds. The interest that you'll have to pay on the loan will certainly wipe out the interest you earn and then some. When the bond matures, you'll have a nice long-term gain. This is a very sound form of conversion. You've used current expenses to wipe out ordinary income, and you find a long-term capital gain at the end of the trail.

There is a definite risk to this. The bond may go sour because the corporation or government that issued it may go broke. That means you have to pick the bond wisely and keep a close eye on it. There is also the unanswerable question of what inflation will do to the dollars you'll get when the bond reaches maturity. That's *always* a problem in any long-term plan.

The remaining strategies are all designed to balance your tax rates from year to year. Keep in mind that, in some situations, to smooth your income, you may actually want to recognize gains in this year and losses later.

▶ **YEAR-END RECOGNITION OF LOSSES**

The simplest strategy of general significance is the recognition of losses at the end of the year. Let's suppose you have losses in stocks that you've held for long or short terms and you nevertheless really believe in the stock. In this situation, it is *always* a good idea to sell the stock, take the loss, reduce your taxable income, and buy the stock back in the next year.

If all other things are equal, it's better to do this with stocks that you've held short-term rather than long-term. That's because the tax laws allow short-term losses to be deducted on a dollar-for-dollar basis from other income up to a limit of $3,000 per year. Long-term holdings that you sell at a loss may be deducted from taxable income on a much less favorable basis. For every dollar of long-term loss that you take, you can deduct only 50 cents from other income. Moreover, the $3,000 limit still applies. That means you need $6,000 of long-term losses to reduce your income by $3,000. You only need $3,000 of short-term losses to reach the same happy result.

If you do plan to sell your losers at the end of a year and repurchase them in the next year, there is one rule that you have to respect. It is the 30-day "wash-sale" rule. The wash-sale rule is designed to prevent people from recognizing losses and then leaping right back into the stock. You simply have to wait until the thirty-first day following the sale to repurchase the stock. The rule works in reverse too. If you *buy* more stock, *then* sell the old stock within 30 days, you cannot recognize the loss on the old stock either.

If you want to be cute (and greedy), you can avoid the wash sale rules with carefully timed sales and repurchase arrangements that brokers have perfected. These deals can work, but in most cases, the thirty-day limitation has no significant effect on the value of the stock. For that reason, it's generally not worth it to try to circumvent the rule. Instead, go with the pros. Sell your losers, and buy different but similar stocks, right away. These are known as "tax swaps" on Wall Street. Wall Street gets drunk on them right around Christmas year after year.

There are two more strategies that people use to favorably arrange their gains and losses in securities transactions. One is called the "straddle" to manufacture short-term losses. The other is called the "short sale against the box."

▶ **STRADDLES**

The securities straddle sounds complicated because it involves some terms from the world of securities, but it's really very simple. A straddle is a short-term transaction in which you simultaneously purchase a contract to buy a stock at a later date (known as a "call") and a contract to sell the same stock at a later date (known as a "put").

The put is one "leg" of the straddle and the call is the other "leg." The trick is to sell whichever end of the deal declines in value at the end of the tax year.

Let's suppose you purchase a put and a call in Fred's Storm Door Company stock in October. If Fred's stock goes up in value, the call becomes more valuable and the put declines in value. You sell the put in late December for less than you paid for it and get a short-term capital loss up to $3,000. You sell the call in the next year for a gain.

If the stock declines in value, you reverse the transaction. You sell the call before the year ends, take the loss, and sell the put at the beginning of the next year.

To construct a successful straddle, you need a competent broker who can find good puts and calls at the right prices. Make sure not to pay too large a commission. Commissions on puts and calls can eat you alive.

Can you hold the leg that increases in value until it qualifies for treatment as a long-term gain? Practically never. Virtually no put or call has a life over nine months. It's probably best to sell the winning leg in the new year, take the guaranteed gain and find a new way to protect it from the Tax Man.

As an alternative to what we've just described, you could replace the leg on which you took a loss with another leg. If you sold the put at a loss, buy a new put in the new year. We don't recommend this because it has attracted hostile attention from the IRS, but it is a good way to support accountants and lawyers to champion your cause.

▶ SHORT SALES AGAINST THE BOX

The final transaction is the short sale against the box. On paper this looks like a very complicated transaction. It isn't.

In a short sale against the box, you freeze the nature of your gain or loss and can pick the time when you realize it. Let's say you own some of Fred's stock and it has appreciated tremendously in value. You believe that Fred's stock is going to collapse, but you don't want to take a gain this year because it will foul up your tax situation. By entering into a short sale against the box, you may contract to take the gain next year. The nature of the gain does not change. A short-term gain remains a short-term gain; and, of course, a long-term gain can't become a short-term gain. The only thing that changes is *when* you take the gain, but *when* can be very important to all of us cash-method taxpayers.

There's a simpler way to reach the same goal. If Fred's stock has a market in puts, buy one that expires next year. The put and the gain will neutralize each other. You can sell both next year when you want to show the gain. Puts are almost always cheaper than short sales against the box. If the stock surprises you and goes up, the put will decline in value. Then, you can use it to offset the gain that you didn't want to take.

This is a popular and useful strategy, but you'll want professional guidance before you make it your own. Have a very competent broker handle this.

This chapter concludes our review of strategies open to small and large investors. In our next chapter, we take you on a tour of the structures inhabited by wealthy investors: the public tax shelters.

CHAPTER..... *Twelve*

▶ | 12 | PUBLIC

TAX

SHELTERS

I got to get some shelter or I'm gonna fade away.

M. JAGGER

THE STRATEGIES discussed in this chapter are offered by brokerage firms to the public at large. Because they are marketed commercially and anyone may sign up (if they have the necessary stake), these ventures are regulated by the Securities Exchange Commission, an agency of the federal government. That keeps them clean, mostly.

The SEC is tough as agencies go. Its job is to make sure that the information contained in these public offerings is accurate and complete, so that investors will not be accidentally or intentionally misled by the people who organize these enterprises. The penalties for spreading misinformation are harsh, and the brokers and entrepreneurs are generally pretty careful to toe the line.

Unfortunately, the SEC and the securities laws guarantee only that the information published about these shelters is accurate and complete. They do not warrant that the shelter is fairly constructed, profitable, or interesting.

In fact, the offering materials tend to be very painfully boring. It is difficult to slog through and make sense of them. The promoters really hope you won't read them. Fight back! Read the materials. Ask your broker a lot of hard questions. He's getting paid for it, and it's your money. Once you part with it, you are reduced to the status of the deaf, dumb, and blind.

These shelters have very little value for most investors. For the most part, they are expensive and dangerously speculative kinds of investments. We've devoted enough time to them so you know how they work. You should see a reputable broker for more information if you're rich enough (or crazy enough) to get involved in them.

All of these shelters share several features. They invite you to participate in conventional commercial and industrial enterprises; they require a good-sized stake to climb inside; they usually provide large above-the-line tax writes-offs during the period of participation, mostly in the form of depreciation allowances (or depreciation's siblings, cost recovery and depletion); they are designed to be profitable on paper but the likelihood of actual profit is low, and if they are profitable, they pay off in large amounts, causing investors in them to scurry around to find a new shelter.

Early in this primer we described them as gilded treadmills, and we'll stick by that characterization. These shelters protect you from the IRS until you choose to climb out or are forced to as a result of the terms of the participation. We'll discuss several types here:

- ☐ the real estate investment syndicate;
- ☐ the research and development syndicate;
- ☐ the motion picture syndicate;
- ☐ the equipment-leasing syndicate;
- ☐ the oil and gas syndicate; and
- ☐ the cattle-breeding syndicate.

► **REAL ESTATE SYNDICATES**

The real estate syndicate is the only one that probably has real value for the investor who is looking for ways to defer liability and convert ordinary income into capital gains. In large part, this is due to the absurdly favorable treatment of improved new and used real estate under the new tax laws. For some technical reasons that we're going to deftly avoid discussing here, residential real estate is in general more favorably treated in the tax laws than commercial real estate.

There is a short explanation for the favored status of real estate: lobbyists. Thanks to lobbyists, the probability is extremely good that you will receive very little or no ordinary income when you decide to sell your share in the syndicate. Instead, if you picked a good investment, you will probably collect a capital gain from the sale, which is taxed much more favorably than ordinary income. The other syndicates that follow can and often do produce large amounts of ordinary income.

There is another atypical benefit of real estate syndicates. Investors do not have to be personally liable for loans used to acquire the real estate. In the other syndicates, investors must generally be personally "at risk" on loans that fuel the investment. The result is that investors in real estate syndicates may claim deductions for funds borrowed from a lender or a seller of the real estate desperate enough to finance the transaction over time and use those loans to acquire depreciation deductions.

As a result of these rules, the investors may take depreciation deductions that significantly exceed the investor's stake and the ordinary income received by the syndicate. A four-to-one ratio of the deductions to the actual investment is common in these syndicates over the life of the venture. Needless to say, this can produce a sizable reduction in the investor's taxable income. And, the investor need not be personally at risk for funds borrowed to finance the syndicate's acquisition.

The basic transaction usually involves a syndicated purchase of a large apartment building. To use a fairly extreme case, the public might invest $500,000 and a bank might lend $2.5 million. The investors may claim depreciation deductions based on the full $3 million, which can be completely written off over fifteen years, at the rate of $\frac{1}{15}$ per year or some faster different formula. If it's done at the rate of $\frac{1}{15}$ per year, the investors divide $140,000 per year of depreciation deductions plus the other expenses of operating and maintaining the building. They get to do this despite investing only $500,000 of their money in the syndicate.

When the property is sold, the result will be a capital gain that equals the resale price minus the depreciated value of the building at the time it's resold, but only if the partnership used straight-line depreciation. This is the classic use of real estate to convert ordinary income into long-term capital gains that we discussed in Chapter Two. Any other rate of depreciation can result in treating much of the gains on sale as ordinary income. That will hurt.

In addition, the force of inflation befriends the investor, because the investors pick up the full amount of any increase in the value of the real estate. The bank gets its loan back, with the contractual interest it earned during the term of the loan. That's all the bank gets; everything else—benefits and burdens—belongs to the investors.

Now we'll move along to the other syndicates. We'll spend less time on them because they're far more speculative and pricey. We suggest that you avoid them.

► **RESEARCH AND DEVELOPMENT SYNDICATES**

These syndicates are designed to raise money to finance advanced research and development ("R and D") projects. These have little value to anyone other than the very rich and the corporate investor.

The short-run benefit is that any R and D expenses can be

deducted from the investor's ordinary income. The long-run benefit is that profits from patents and products that are developed and sold by the syndicate may be taxed as capital gains. It is depressing that such important activities get such a relatively small boost from Congress. Blame it on the lobbyists.

► **MOTION PICTURE SYNDICATES**

These are of equally dubious value. They come in any number of packages and wrappings, but the basic idea remains the same. The public invests in the production or distribution (or both) of a film that is almost invariably produced by the promoters of the syndicate or their friends. The investors may usually claim an investment tax credit in addition to the other expenses of the syndicate.

The risks are substantial and the benefits limited. The film may not make any money, and movies that bomb have minimal salvage value. Moreover, you can only claim deductions to the extent of your investment and for loans for which you are really on the hook. These are complicated and very risky investments; leave them to the folks who wear open-necked shirts and gold chains and "take" meetings.

► **EQUIPMENT-LEASING SYNDICATES**

The idea here is that the investors purchase industrial equipment like tanker-trailers and boxcars and then lease them. The investors can collect large investment tax credits and offset their income with operating expenses and depreciation. The deductions can be in excess of investment but, to claim depreciation, the investors must be personally liable on any loans they used to finance the purchases.

In recent years, investors have been burned badly by boxcar deals. Among other problems, railroad stock tends to get stolen. This deal is for the stouthearted. Or the mutton-headed.

► **OIL AND GAS SYNDICATES**

These shelters are very popular, but investors don't always understand them well. The key economic feature is that investors can take a lot of deductions in the years when the syndicate is exploring and drilling. If the syndicate loses money, the investors get to deduct any resulting losses. The investors do not get to deduct losses financed by borrowed funds unless they are personally liable on the loans.

If the drilling produces oil, the investors can make unbelievable profits. The investors then may profitably sell their shares for enormous but favorably taxed capital gains.

Of course the drilling may produce nothing but air, sand, or water. If there is no strike, the investors' losses are limited to the amount of investment and personal liabilities for borrowed funds. That means the investors may have to pay off loans they always thought of as a lot of legal clutter at the bottom of the signature page. The public has been treated to some nasty education about that clutter lately.

These investments offer huge and early deductions and present the possibility of spectacular profits. The risks of total loss are equally large. These aren't logical investments for most of us.

► CATTLE-BREEDING SYNDICATES

Promoters of these deals sell shares in ventures to raise and slaughter cattle for profit or to develop new breeds for the same purpose. The tax advantages are straightforward. Investors get to deduct substantial feeding expenses, but these benefits have been reduced by recent Congressional legislation that has shrunk allowances for deductible expenses.

There are multiple risks. Cattle prices fluctuate wildly, and a herd may be wiped out by disease or terrible weather. A new breed may be an unmarketable genetic bust. You can insure yourself against an unproductive breed, or destruction of the herd, but you can't control cattle prices.

The worst aspect of these deals is that income from the syndicates is ordinary. This is not an investment that directly produces capital gains. You may sell your share of the parent cattle to get a capital gain, but their offspring create ordinary income. Dubious offspring.

Well. That completes our brief review of shelters. It's about time to close up shop. But first, we'll talk about charity.

CHAPTER

13 CHARITABLE

CONTRIBUTIONS

━━━━━━━━━━━━━━━

In necessary things, unity; in doubtful things, liberty;
in all things, charity.

R. BAXTER

━━━━━━━━━━━━━━━

You've probably heard that
making charitable contributions will reduce your income taxes.
Although that's true, you have to part with actual wealth to get
any tax benefits. Moreover, recent amendments to the tax laws
will keep these amounts in flux for the next few years.

► **SOME GENERAL RULES**

Until very recently, charitable contributions were purely itemized
(below-the-line) deductions. Moreover, in most cases, you could
deduct no more than 50% of your adjusted gross income for
charitable contributions. Consequently, your contributions had tax
value only if the deductible percentage of your contribution plus
your other itemized deductions exceeded the zero-bracket amount
for your filing status. To reduce your taxes, you had to make very
large charitable contributions (which most of us can't do) or be
able to throw them in the itemized stew with a potload of medical
expenses, interest expenses, and so forth.

In all likelihood, they were classified as itemized deductions
because Congress wanted to protect us from economic ruin
through typically American acts of unqualified generosity.

Early in Ronald Reagan's administration, Congress changed
the rules governing charitable contributions. Essentially, Congress
added a five-year schedule during which charitable contributions
will gradually become nonitemized (above-the-line) deductions
without upper limits for all taxpayers. The change is very slow in
the first year; if you don't itemize, you'll be able to deduct above the
line 25% of $100 of your contributions or $25, whichever is
greater. The percentages and dollar amounts increase steadily
during the following years. In the last year of the schedule, you
will be able to deduct 100% of your contribution above the line,
without any limit, even if you don't itemize. You'll be interested to

know that these provisions expire in the year that follows. Charitable contributions make the kids in Congress very uneasy.

After reading this, you may question whether it's strategically sound to make charitable contributions. Unfortunately, the short answer is, "Usually no."

Still, there are times when you can save a great deal of money with contributions that are properly designed to reduce their cost. There are even cases where a charitable contribution can be personally beneficial. There are several excellent ways to support your favorite charities and reduce your taxes.

► **GIFTS OF PROPERTY**

The first and simplest method involves gifts of property that have increased in value. The tax laws treat favorably gifts of appreciated assets that have been held for more than one year.

Suppose you want to make a gift of $100 to the ASPCA. You hold a share of stock that you bought two years ago for $20 and is now worth $100. Do you sell the stock and give the proceeds to charity? No! If you sell the stock first, you will have to pay a capital gains tax that could be as much as $16 if you're in the 50% bracket (50% of 40% of your $80 capital gain). That means you'd have to scare up another $16 to make your $100 contribution and get a $100 deduction.

Instead, if you give the share of stock to the charity, you get a $100 deduction. Structurally, this is identical to giving gifts to persons in lower brackets to reduce your tax rates. Do *not* prearrange a sale of stock, because the IRS will nail the capital gain to your income.

As always, there are other limitations on this but they are easy to sort out. If you held the share for less than one year, you can only take the cost that you paid for the property as a deduction, because gifts of assets yielding short-term capital gains are handled that way. It's the law. Period. A similar result will occur if you try to give away an asset that produces ordinary income. For example, if you own a grocery store, and give a case of beans to charity, you can't deduct the retail price of the beans. You're obliged to use a specific formula that produces a smaller deductible amount.

Unhappily, the laws are also relatively hostile to gifts of property that are unrelated to the charity's activities or purposes. Don't give the Mona Lisa to the Scouts, no matter how much you want to help.

So, if you want to make a charitable gift, choose an asset that you have held for investments for more than a year, such as stocks or bonds, or give away tangible property that the charity can use. Give the Mona Lisa to the Biloxi Museum of Art.

► **THE HEAVY STUFF: CONSERVATION EASEMENTS AND CHARITABLE REMAINDERS**

The subject of charitable contributions becomes more elegant when you talk about real estate or income-producing property. If you make contributions of these kinds of assets to appropriate recipients, you can do it with virtually no personal discomfort.

There are two basic ways to do this. The first method is to make a contribution of some property that you know the charity will use in a way that protects or enhances the personal (not economic) value of your other assets. The second method is to contribute something that you won't be around to use.

► **GIFTS OF "EASEMENTS"**

The most striking example of the first method is the charitable gift of "conservation easements." An "easement" is an archaic real estate term that described a right to use your real estate in a certain way or a limitation on the way you can use it.

For example, assume that you own a farm next to a road. If you sell to someone part of the farm that has no access to the road, your buyer will want an easement to use your land to get to the inaccessible land. You sell to the buyer the easement to use your land. The Code permits you to give easements to charitable organizations and deduct from your income the fair market value of the easement, which is the appraised amount by which the easement reduces the value of your property.

Here are some examples of what you may do. You can give to your qualified local charitable conservation society or to a local government the right to ban development of your property. Or, you can give to your city's historical preservation society the right to preserve historic features of your home's exterior.

In its most clever form, you can use conservation easements to protect the character of vacation property. Let's suppose you own a vacation home in a lovely forest at some distance from the nasty city where you live and work. You want to make sure that your part of forest retains its pleasantly primitive character. You may transfer to a local government or qualified conservation charity the right to develop your property and take an immediate deduction for the extent to which the easement diminishes the fair market value of your property. Better still, you can organize all of the other landowners in your neck of the woods to join you in this arrangement. Each of the participating landowners becomes entitled to an immediate deduction for the easement, provided there really is a public benefit.

These easements must be constructed to be irrévocably enforceable against you and all subsequent owners of your land. Lawyers call these "easements in perpetuity."

The happy results? You get to reduce your tax bill and ensure that your vacation home will retain its attractive character to the limits of imperfect human law and changing social rules. Furthermore, your local real estate taxes should drop, since they are usually based on the value of the land as if it were fully developed. Since the land now *can't* be developed, the local taxes go down. If your taxes don't go down, get mad.

PRESERVING THE HISTORIC FEATURES OF YOUR HOME'S EXTERIOR

► **GIFTS OF "REMAINDERS"**

If you want to go a step further than easements, you may give a "remainder" interest in a farm or your personal residence. In this situation, you make a gift of property that becomes effective when you, your spouse, or some other living person dies. When all the appropriate persons have passed away, the charitable organization or governmental body receives the full title to the property. In the meantime, you take a charitable deduction. You cannot do this if you want the property to continue as part of your family's estate through subsequent generations.

For example, you own a farm. You want to give it to the Audobon Society, but you want your living children to have the use of the property after you and your spouse die. You deed the property to the Society but the deed specifies that you, your spouse, and your named children will have the exclusive right to make modest use of the property until you have all passed away.

The transfer to the Society is an immediately deductible charitable contribution, but it is *not* equal to the current fair market value of the farm. The value of the contribution is reduced by your exclusive use of the farm for the specified term. The reduction in the value of the gift is determined by reference to some complicated actuarial tables published by the Treasury.

This transaction cries out for a competent advisor. You will need someone skilled in the ins and outs of real estate law and the attendant tax computations.

► **CHARITABLE GIFTS OF OTHER PROPERTY**

We mentioned a second and analogous method for charitable contributions: you may contribute income-producing property but retain the income (or a portion of it) during your lifetime (or your lifetime plus some other living person or persons).

There are various forms that this gift can take. Two of them—the "charitable remainder annuity trust" and the "charitable remainder uni-trust"—are for the very wealthy. You can learn about them when you're rich enough to throw this book away. The legal and accounting fees that go into their construction are prohibitive costs for all but the very rich.

Instead, we'll look at the "pooled income fund." For all practical purposes, it is a mutual fund run by a charitable organization.

If you want to participate, you transfer property to the fund. You can even transfer appreciated assets to the fund without paying capital gains tax on the transfer. In exchange for the gift, you get an itemized deduction equal to the value of the property at the estimated time of your death or the death of the last person you've named as entitled to the use of the property. The fund pays you an annual return based on the performance of its portfolio and the size of your contribution.

You can measure the value of the gift in a fairly straightforward way. First, determine how much you're contributing to the pooled income fund. Let's suppose you're giving a $10,000 asset to the fund. Using the Treasury's Extremely Boring Actuarial Tables, the EBATs, determine the total number of years during which you and the other named living person can expect to receive that income. Multiply the number of years by the annual return on the contribution and subtract that amount from the value of the gift, using tables and interest rate assumptions in the EBATs. The net remainder is the amount of the charitable contribution that you may deduct this year. Extremely bored? Confused? Don't worry, the charity will do it for you. They have stables of EBAT experts.

There are two outcomes here. One affects your taxes and the other affects your overall economic position.

From a tax standpoint, you get the benefits of a deduction for a charitable contribution; you also receive a stream of taxable income from the fund. The size of the deduction varies with the length of the term during which you receive the fund's income. If you are comparatively young and the other named beneficiaries are young, the period of income is larger and the deduction is smaller.

You part with ownership of the property you give away, but your income from the fund is based on the value of your contribution at the time of the gift, rather than the value of the deduction or the changing value of the gift. By the way, if you contribute appreciated stock, that does you no harm.

From an economic point of view, you are usually better off hanging onto your property and directly earning income from it. You may make better decisions about its use than the fund's managers, who must be fairly conservative and rarely produce a very high rate of return. On the other hand, you're placing the property in the hands of professional managers who work with a diversified portfolio that may provide you a steadier and more predictable return. Moreover, you get to help your favorite charity build a better economic foundation for its worthy activities. If you are in a high income year, it can level your income, always an admirable goal.

It's an interesting process. You have the satisfaction of knowing that your property will go to a charity at your death. You can also derive comfort from knowing that you've created that arrangement without a significant loss of income during your lifetime.

Many charitable organizations also operate a variant of the pooled income fund called the "charitable annuity" program. In conjunction with an insurance company, the charity offers annuity contracts that you can buy in various amounts. The contract then begins to pay you income for life when you reach a certain age. You also receive an itemized deduction for the part of the amount you pay into the program.

The deduction is calculated in roughly the same way as it is for pooled income funds. Suppose you purchase a lifetime annuity for $20,000. The annuity contract promises to pay you $100 a month for the rest of your life. If the EBATs set your life expectancy at ten years from the starting date of the annuity payments, the value of the annuity is $12,000. You receive an immediate charitable deduction of $8,000, which is essentially the *cost* to you of the annuity minus its *value* to you.

▶ **WARNING: TWO "CHARITABLE" SHELTERS THAT ARE FRAUDULENT**

Number One: The Phony Charitable "Gift"

In the area of charitable contributions—like most other areas of taxation—the IRS is willing to let you get something for something. You may receive a favorable tax benefit by making a real gift. The Service does *not* like to allow the deduction when you try to get something for nothing.

With pathetic frequency, taxpayers have tried to milk the deduction for charitable contributions. There is one particularly foolish scheme that confidence artists successfully use to separate taxpayers from their dollars. This particular scam is generally marketed door to door, and you should welcome its purveyors as you would rabid dogs.

You are solicited to purchase bibles, jewelry, or the like, and advised to hold the property for a year and a day. Then you donate it to the charity of your choice, claim that the property has appreciated phenomenally (three or four times its original cost to you) during the year, and try to deduct the alleged value of the gift.

The IRS won't even bother to respect you for your ingenuity. Instead, it will properly assert that the marketplace does not work like that. The Service will promptly reduce the deductible amount of the contribution to a much more modest appreciated value or to the price that you paid for the artifact.

These tricksters are perpetrating a fraud. Don't become a victim of it.

Number Two: The Tax-exempt "Church"

The other species of fraud is the phony church. If we remember right, this became very popular in the late sixties, a period in which a lot of other things became popular, even Richard Nixon and lentil soup.

The church gambit is based on the fact that federal, state, and local governments may not tax churches. In elementary civics we all learned that the United States Constitution erected a wall between the Church and the State. Churches are given tax-exempt status. Contributions to them are charitable contributions, subject to the rules we discussed.

Because governments cannot tax churches, some subnormal mutation of American ingenuity said, "Well, gosh! I'll jist become a church and never have to pay no taxes no how!" And he became a church and he begat other churches who begat other churches.

The process is simple. A "parent" church organization sells a charter and some basic tax advice to you. In turn, you sign various documents that purport to convert you into a church, often with some ridiculous name like the Bubbling Well Church of Eternal Joy. Honest.

Anyway, you sign over all of your income to the church or you make a contract with the church to provide various services to it. The church then "leases" your services to the public. You and your family take a vow of poverty, and you turn your home into a chapel, your car into a clerical coach, your children into cherubs, and your spouse into a sacristan.

When an IRS agent comes to your "church" to inquire politely about the whereabouts of your taxes, you claim that your income is not taxable because the income belongs to the church and the government can't tax churches. You also claim that your meals and lodging are not income because you're performing services around the church. You might as well try to sell the agent some religious artifacts during the visit, because you'll need the money to pay your tax bill, your accountant, your lawyer, and (unlikely but always possible) your bail bondsman.

The only way the church-as-shelter works is if you are sincere about it. The government will respect it if you're on the level (and you have our best wishes). If you're not, forget it.

That wraps up charity, which begins and usually ends at home. We'll end with The Meaning Of It All.

PHONY CHURCHES

Epilogue

THE

MEANING

OF

IT

ALL

IN THIS PRIMER, we've tried to show you how to use the tax laws to your advantage. The laws are shaped by the economic conditions and social values that dominate our culture.

The business of America is still business. It's unlikely that the tax laws will reflect any big changes in the near future. Instead, the middle class will continue to get soaked because they are so easy to tax. Most of them are employees whose salaries and wages can be assessed with ease before they get their checks.

There is a lot of debate over various alternatives to progressive taxation. We doubt the laws will change to tax individuals and businesses on a flat rate.

Even if they do, we believe that much of what we've said here will remain relevant. The laws will still favor businesses. In some form or other, the rules will still recognize and favor deductions for profit-oriented expense and capital gains over ordinary income.

We hope you understand that our tax laws reflect the values of the people who run the American shop and shape American opinion. Depending on your point of view, this can be a reassuring or frightening notion.

We end with three warnings and some advice.

First, we pay a hidden price for inequities in our tax structure. The tax laws favor the powerful and the wealthy more than they ever have since World War II. For one thing, the top tax rates have dropped from over 90% to 50%.

To some extent, the tax laws support investments and labor that are economically and socially productive, but we are a long way from a well-ordered set of tax laws and may never have them. The kind of current legislative insanity that gives technological development a smaller tax benefit than used real estate will still go on. Don't be naive when you read and hear government officials and special interest groups. Take the advice of Bertrand Russell—be skeptical. Find ways to support your own group's interests. That probably means forcing changes in lobbying and campaign financing systems.

That's our first warning. Our second warning concerns the IRS. The Service is composed of all kinds of people. Like every other agency, it is a mix of efficient and inefficient, cruel and compassionate people. It also has enormous power. The government wants its bill collectors to collect the bills. Don't go out of your way to engage them in combat.

Our last warning is closely related to the other two. Over the years, many courageous and principled people have refused to pay all or some portion of their taxes as a way to protest inequities in the tax laws or our general governmental operation. Unethical hucksters have even made money counseling them to do so. Tax protesters almost always lose. In fact, even taxpayers who pay their taxes but challenge government expenditures in lawsuits are usually blown out of court.

At your own peril, then, you may refuse to pay your taxes or challenge the process in a lawsuit. The odds that you will lose in the short run are overwhelming. You may draw public or governmental attention to inequities and you may spur reform, but don't delude yourself. You will pay for your decisions.

Our final remark is repetitive. To minimize your taxes you need two things. The first is personal discipline. Take action early and thoughtfully, and do more than just hunt down deductions. Instead, you want to level your income, convert current deductions into capital gains (in the real estate depreciation game especially), defer income if your rates are stable, and split income with others, be they friends, family, or corporations. The second thing you need is an economic stake. Save some money, if you possibly can. Only that way can you begin to navigate freely in these tricky waters. It means you can start an IRA, or maybe buy some depreciable property. Then you can apply your discipline.

We've come to the end of our time together. We hope we've explained to you some of the mysteries wrought in the name of the Old Sixteenth. We also hope we've enabled you to dance the Tax Dance a bit more gracefully. The rest, gentle reader, (of course and as always) is up to you.

Index

▶

▶ A   ▶ B

▶ C   ▶ D

▶ E   ▶ F

▶ H   ▶ I

▶ J   ▶ L

▶ M   ▶ N

▶ O   ▶ P

▶ R   ▶ S

▶ T   ▶ U

▶ V   ▶ W

▶ Z